My Life is Just Speech Material…
And, So is Yours

A Guide to What to Say and How to Say It

Tammy A. Miller

My Life is Just Speech Material…
And, So is Yours

A Guide to What to Say and How to Say It

Tammy A. Miller, MA, DTM

First Edition
ISBN 978-0-9701379-6-8
EAN 978097013968

Hugz and Company
Lighthearted Press

Cover Photo by Tiffany Dawn Earnest
Tiffany Dawn Designs^C
www.tiffanydawndesigns.com

Fashion Designs by Lacey J. Earnest

Cover Design by Heather Harpster

For information, please contact:
Tammy A. Miller
E-mail: tammy@tammyspeaks.com
Web Site: www.tammyspeaks.com
(814) 360-4031

Dear Lord,
Please use me this day
Beyond my wildest dreams

Table of Contents

Acknowledgments 6

What People Are Saying… 8

Foreword 11

My Path to This Book 13

Chapter One...14

  It's All Speech Material 14

Chapter Two...18

  Your Own Speech Cookie© 18

    Notes and Key Points From This Chapter.............25

Chapter Three 26

  Think in Threes..26

    Notes and Key Points From This Chapter.............29

Chapter Four 30

  Purposeful Presenting 30

    Notes and Key Points From This Chapter.............43

Chapter Five...44

  Success in Life 44

    Notes and Key Points From This Chapter: 50

Chapter Six 51

  Sharing Challenges 51

    Notes and Key Points From This Chapter.............57

Chapter Seven 58

  Lessons Along the Journey of Life 58

    Notes and Key Points From This Chapter.............62

Chapter Eight 63

  People I Have Met 63

    Notes and Key Points From This Chapter.............66

Chapter Nine 67

  Speechwriting – Dolly Style 67

    Notes and Key Points From This Chapter.............72

Chapter Ten 73

  Lessons From the Animal Kingdom.........................73

    Notes and Key Points From This Chapter.............79

Chapter Eleven 80

  Funny Stories Make Great Material 80

    Notes and Key Points From This Chapter.............89

Chapter Twelve 90
   Just to Quote a Few 90
      Notes and Key Points From This Chapter..............96
Chapter Thirteen 97
   Fortune Cookie 97
      Notes and Key Points From This Chapter.............101
Chapter Fourteen 102
   Look Around the Room.................................102
      Notes and Key Points From This Chapter.............105
Chapter Fifteen 106
   Random Thoughts to Real Life Talks 106
      Notes and Key Points From This Chapter.............110
Chapter Sixteen 111
   The Basic Structure 111
      Introduction 112
      Body...117
      Conclusion 122
      Notes and Key Points From This Chapter.............130
Chapter Seventeen 131
   A Variety of Structures.................................131
      Notes and Key Points From This Chapter.............136
Chapter Eighteen 137
   Image Mapping for Presenters 137
      Notes and Key Points From This Chapter.............142
Chapter Nineteen 143
   Mapping Your Talk 143
Chapter Twenty..148
   Tiers to Talking 148
Top 10 List – Before You Speak 152
      Notes and Key Points From This Chapter.............154
Please Hand Me the Microphone........................155
Resource Section 157
   Notes 160

Acknowledgments

This book has my name on the front cover but it is truly God's project. Thank you Lord for the wonderful blessings that have accompanied this book and the fantastic people I have met along the path to my life as speech material. Always keep me mindful of the daily blessings and Proverbs 3:5-6 on this great adventure of life!

To my beautiful mother, Ruth – my biggest cheerleader. I am clearly her favorite daughter, and both my brothers know it! I am so proud to be your daughter! Thank you for giving me speeches about family and love.

To Tiffany and Lacey for giving me unlimited material as I have watched you grow into the most incredible young women. I am so proud to be your Mom! Thank you for so many presentation topics relating to children, growing up, road trips, great adventures, challenges, laughter and especially love.

To my family, Jim, Jimmy, Mike, and Angie for your limitless support of all of the crazy things I do. Your inspiration has led me to a wide range of presentations – serious, funny and everything in between.

To Mary for being my sanity check (or is that insanity check?). You have given me great material on friendship, crazy times and furniture shopping antics (yes, it is Mary's story mentioned in Chapter One ☺).

To Bill for sharing in our many great adventures along the highway (it is his head, and the flying deer, in the convertible with the top down, and lots of laughter in Chapter One ☺).

To Maggie, Molly, Tyke and Bailey for unconditional love. Chapter Ten is dedicated to you.

To Dr. B for saving my life so I could go on living, loving and laughing. As the head of my Humor Team, you gave me speeches on surviving, daring to try new things, and the value of asking questions about my healthcare, okay, okay, LOTS of questions!

To my team of editors – Ruth, Mary, Linda, Kathy and Tina - you ladies have made me look better and if we have missed any typos, I take full responsibility!

To my long list of friends who have shared my life and provided a lot of great speech material over the years. I am so blessed to call each of you my friend!

To Lorie of "Secrets By Lorie" for giving me my fabulous razzle-dazzle eyes and wonderful presentations on The Benefits of Permanent Make-Up, and my first tattoos!

To Ted, Craig, Dilip, Dan, Anita, Sheryl, Diane, Linda, Rebecca, Helen, Kathy, Lance, and Gavin for your kind words. You have touched my heart more than you may have realized!

To the many, many Toastmasters who have crossed my path, impacted my life, and given me speech material. Toastmasters is a wonderful place to start as you learn that success comes step by step.

To my fellow speakers of life's material in the National Speakers Association (NSA) and the Association for Applied and Therapeutic Humor (AATH). This is a wonderful business we are in, and I thank you for your friendships and fellowship as we find more ways to make a difference.

What People Are Saying...

(Check out the Resource Section in the back of the book for additional contact information for many of these people.)

What people are saying about **"My Life is Just Speech Material, and So is Yours"**, and this author.....

"What good is a diamond nobody can see? What good is a great idea that fails due to a lack of clarity and less than effective communication? In order to influence others to take your desired next step, you must master both planned and impromptu presentations. Professional Speech Coach Tammy Miller will help you build your masterpieces by using the information in this valuable book. The OREO Formula by itself will instantly raise your profile as an excellent presenter whose value will be rewarded time and time again."
Craig Valentine
1999 World Champion of Public Speaking
Author of **World Class Speaking** and **The Nuts and Bolts of Public Speaking**

"Tammy Miller has so many traits and talents for which to be admired. She is one of the 'Givers' of this world -- always giving blessings to others. I know Tammy as a top notch public speaker and trainer, and more importantly, a loving, caring individual who has had the wisdom to learn from life's hard knocks and then use those lessons to reach and teach others. The readers of this book are very fortunate to get a glimpse into the heart and humor of Tammy Miller!"
Dilip R. Abayasekara, Ph.D., Accredited Speaker
Past International President, Toastmasters International

"Tammy Miller is a phenomenal speaker, trainer and writer. She combines humorous life experiences with real life lessons, creating a unique connection with her audience."
Daniel Rex, Executive Director
Toastmasters International

"Like a flashlight on a treasure hunt, Tammy leads us to discover the joy and creativity hidden within ourselves."
Anita Thies
Author of **The Joyful Journey of Nursing Home Clowning** and Chair of the Caring Clown Committee of the World Clown Association

My Life is Just Speech Material, and, So is Yours is a must-have resource, with easy-to-follow tips anyone can use, and written in a lively and down-to-earth conversational tone! Just learning the Speech Cookie method is worth buying the book! This is a novel and memorable approach to having more credibility through framework of responses."
Sheryl Roush, President/CEO Sparkle Presentations, Inc. Professional Speaker and Coach

"Tammy grabs our attention right from the start, holds us captive till the end, and leaves us wanting more! Her humor and "down-to-earth" motivational messages makes us believe that we can do anything. Everyone should have Tammy's outlook on life!"
Diane M. Brown
Penn State University Professional Development Trainer

"Tammy has taken the guesswork and pain out of presentation and speech writing with her thought-provoking guide to presentations based on life. Cleverly broken into chapters that reference experiences that each person can recognize in some way, the book provides clear examples and a presentation development guide to help new and experienced speakers focus their thoughts. I won't give another presentation without taking a look at this guide for ideas, encouragement and focus."
Linda Young
Life Traveler Extraordinaire

"*Learn from a Pro! You will never again struggle on a topic for a speech. In this book, Tammy Miller provides useful and practical exercises to extract speech topics from your every day life.*"
Rebecca Lamperski
Author of **In Full Bloom**

"*In her refreshing style, Tammy Miller gives intriguing strategies for impromptu speaking to formal presentations. This easy-to-use guide offers confidence and success in all speaking situations.*"
Helen Blanchard, DTM
Toastmasters International President 1985-86

"*WOW! Tammy has done it again. This book is easy to follow and understand, and her Speech Cookie concept is just brilliant. I will never look at impromptu communication the same way. Excellent!*"
Kathy Salloum
Public Relations Director

"*Tammy Miller brings the experience to stage of a person who has lived life and understands how to deal with and find the value in the trials and adversity we all face.*"
Lance Miller
2005 World Champion of Public Speaking

"*Tammy is an inspiration - both as a person and as a speaker. She really connects with her audience through her warm and engaging presentation style. I highly recommend this book and her services to you.*"
Gavin Blakey
Past International President, Toastmasters International
Brisbane, Australia

Foreword

By, Ted Corcoran
President Toastmasters International 2003/04
Author of *The Leadership Bus*
Dublin, Ireland

In my over twenty years as a Toastmaster, one of the most common remarks by people I have met all over the world was, simply, 'I can't think of anything to write a speech about'. These remarks were made by intelligent and educated people who lived lives full of events and experiences. They were unable to see that every such event and life experience, as well as everything that has ever happened or is happening in the world around us makes wonderful speech material.

Even when ideas present themselves, people often struggle with turning them into speeches that will inform, motivate, persuade, inspire or entertain their audiences. They struggle to find a logical way to present their ideas for maximum effect. Many, many times I've listened to people speaking but not communicating. And, if the speakers fail to get their ideas across to their audiences, then that period of time the speech takes, either long or short, is wasted for both sides.

This workbook by Tammy Miller has the answers. From hundreds of ideas for speeches to different methods for constructing them, Tammy shows us how even the most inexperienced speaker can turn a single idea into a speech/presentation that will impress any audience. Using this workbook as a guide you will be able to take any idea/opinion/fact and build it into an interesting speech which will enable you to communicate effectively and achieve your desired result.

Tammy is a much sought after speaker and presenter herself and brings a deep understanding of the needs of speakers everywhere to the writing of this book. It gives you the basic information to help you write a speech about everything and anything under the sun, organized effectively for maximum impact.

My Path to This Book

I am so excited and blessed that this book project has been completed, and you are holding in your hands a work of passion and love.

- It is designed as a workbook for a specific purpose. I truly want it to be a book that you can wrap your arms around, dog-ear the corners, fill in the spaces, and write in the margins. Make it your own personal working journal filled with wonderfully useful ideas.

After you have completed the exercises in this book, you will have topics for well over 100 presentations. You will have so much material that you will be looking for places to speak - begging people to give you the microphone, practicing in front of the mirror...the dog...to your breakfast cereal...in the park to that statue of a famous person – well, you get the idea.

It doesn't matter if you are giving a formal or informal presentation, asked to speak at a meeting in your workplace or community venue, responding to a job interview question or delivering a full day workshop, this book will help you generate more ideas and ways to deliver the presentation more effectively.

Not only will you have ideas for presentations, but it is my deep desire that the information presented in this book will help you, not just in the area of speaking, but also to be more creative, a better thinker and a better writer. In fact, it is my desire that you will gain skills to help you anywhere that communication is a key to your greater success.

The great aspect about the information presented in this book is that you can use it for as long as you live – literally. It is a true fact, that **My Life is Just Speech Material, but more importantly so is yours!**

Chapter One
It's All Speech Material

Have you ever had "one of those days" when...

- a pipe breaks in the garage and the water is pouring in, but only in a small area... that just happens to be over your boxes of rare books and irreplaceable high school yearbooks? OR...

- your best friend goes a little crazy furniture shopping and says, "Of course, we can get this waterbed in the van",... did I mentioned that there was already a full couch, dresser, and recliner in the van? OR...

- you have traveled several hundred miles on your road trip and you are getting closer to home when that deer darts out from the side, hits your cars, flips over a friends head and the top...of your convertible...top down, of course, and lands beside the road, with a mere $6,000 worth of damage, on a desolate stretch of road near dusk? And we laughed like crazy?! OR...

- you are just 42 years old when the doctor says, "Tammy, I am afraid it is cancer." OR...

- you just can't wait to crawl into bed and get the day over, and then the bed breaks and you find yourself on the floor staring up at the ceiling? OR...

- you are in that job interview for your "dream job" and the question you never expected is asked? You draw a blank and realize at that moment that you have just lost the job opportunity of a lifetime.

I am sure you get the idea, as we have all lived similar events in our lives. These are just a few of the real life experiences that have given life to many of my presentations over the years.

From these examples have come speeches on home safety; preserving your collectibles; the value of friendship; packing valuables in small places; many presentations on dealing with healing and adversity with humor; countless presentations on motivation and goal setting; and the development of a delightful Speech Cookie$^©$.

Yes, my life is just speech material...but most importantly...so is YOURS.

There are two main topics on the minds of most people when they are about to give a speech or presentation:

- What am I going to talk about?

- How am I going to say it?

The goal of this publication is to offer suggestions on improving your impromptu speaking and formal presentations, whether you are a novice speaker or a more experienced speaker looking for ways to fine tune your current skill set.

From the Speech Cookie to help "sweeten" your impromptu communication, to a lot of ways to cultivate new ideas, then several structures to help you make your presentations most effective. This is your personal workbook and topic notebook. Let it work for you to help take your next communication from ordinary to extraordinary.

Everyday life is an education filled with speech material. Look around you and embrace each day. You just never know where the inspiration for your next presentation will come from, or how your next life changing moment can help others. Look around you and live life...love life...and talk about it!

Start With What You Know

The activity on these two pages is designed to give your thinking a jumpstart in the direction of putting a presentation together.

Think about what you already know and could talk about, even if you don't have all of the details for the topic in your mind yet. This is a free thinking brainstorming session just between you and your mind, or maybe engage your family and friends to help you think about what you already know or topics on which you are already passionate.

These topics can be from your experience, hobbies, interests, politics, or favorite books, just to name a few examples. Don't worry if you can't complete all 20 spaces right now. By the end of this book, you will have completed all of these lines, plus many, many more.

1. _____

2. _____

3. _____

4. _____

5. _____

6. _____

7. _____

8. _____

9. _____

10. _____

11. _____

12. _____

13. _____

14. _____

15. _____

16. _____

17. _____

18. _____

19. _____

20. _____

Chapter Two
Your Own Speech Cookie©
(No Calories!)

My very smart mother always taught me to eat my dessert first. She said to go for the sweets at the beginning of the meal because you never know what might happen during dinner. So, let's get started with a very sweet part of speaking.

American writer, Ruth Gordon, once said, "The very best impromptu speeches are the ones written well in advance." For many people, the most difficult type of communication is the impromptu response. Most of us have seen the beautiful, poised young woman standing in her glimmering gown with her hair perfectly coiffed and her make-up just exquisite, when she is asked the question, "What would you do to achieve World Peace"? And, we have often seen the face of this lovely woman suddenly quiver as she realizes THIS question was not among the thousands that she rehearsed, and this may be the moment that determines whether or not she will wear the coveted crown.

Most of us are familiar with this type of question and answer exchange from the world of beauty or scholarship pageants, but it is certainly not reserved for the beauty pageant world. For many of us it is more likely to happen when our boss asks us a question in the middle of the hallway, or we are fielding the question and answer portion of a presentation.

Many of us can relate to this line of questioning when facing a job interview. In the job interview, the way we answer questions can play a key role in determining whether or not we get the job, or how much we will be paid in the position. Just like the pageant questions, there are also multiple lists and books available for sample interview questions that one may be asked in an interview, but these lists do not include every question a person could be asked.

What is most intimidating about this type of communication is that we have not prepared our answers in advance. How can we possibly do this if we don't know the question?

In reality, most of the questions we answer in our lives do not have rehearsed answers, but we can give a BETTER response if we are more prepared. Sound confusing? Prepared for impromptu speaking when you do not know the question in advance? Yes! The same way that a solid speech structure, as we will discuss in later chapters, can help us develop a better speech, a solid *response structure* can help us achieve better results with an impromptu question. How? With a Speech Cookie©!

As children, of all ages, many of us enjoy the yummy goodness of an OREO™ cookie. We have experienced the debate between dunk the whole thing in milk, or separate the cookie part and eat the cream first, or any other way you would like to eat the OREO. The same way a cookie can be made up of different parts, so can an effective response structure for an impromptu question.

Let's borrow the goodness of an OREO to help us with our next impromptu response by turning it into a no-calorie, impromptu, SPEECH COOKIE.

The OREO is made up of two cookies with cream in the middle. Keep this in mind as you recall the value of the Speech Cookie. We will look at the Speech Cookie as a whole cookie, and then look at some examples of how this little tool can help you make a big impression.

In many cases when we are asked a question, we are being asked our opinion. If it is truly a request for our "opinion", then it is what we think about the information being sought in the question. We are not being asked for our co-worker's opinion, or the opinion of our neighbor down the street, but "our" opinion – what do WE think about the subject matter, therefore, the first part of our Speech Cookie is our **OPINION**.

The next two parts of the cookie that make up the "cream" are used to reinforce the **OPINION**. The "R" in our Speech Cookie is **REASON** or **REASONS** to support your opinion.

The second part of the "cream" is **EXAMPLE** or **EXAMPLES** to add additional support to your opinion.

Depending on the time you have to respond, and the nature of the question, you can offer one or more reasons and examples to reinforce your response. One way to look at it is that together, the **REASON(S)** and **EXAMPLE(S)** make up the "double stuff" of the cookie.

Finally, wrap it up by going back to the beginning and stating your **OPINION** once again.

Thus, the Speech Cookie OREO Method[©], that can be used in most situations to respond to an impromptu question looks like this:

Opinion

Reason(s)

Example(s)

Opinion

Let's look at two questions and how we can use the Speech Cookie OREO Method to form a possible response to the questions.

Question: Do you believe that individuals can have a positive impact on the environment?

O - Opinion – Yes, I believe an individual can have a positive impact on the environment.

R - Reason(s) – Each of us can take some action to help make a difference, and have a positive impact, even if it is just in our own home. We may be a single person, yet, if all of us would make small changes, the total impact on the environment would be substantial.

E - Example(s) – An example of this would be to recycle. People can recycle in a lot of different ways, not just in the recycle areas that a lot of communities provide for glass and plastic, but also in the clothing we wear. If we donate used clothing, and buy used clothing from second hand stores, we reduce the need for more clothing to be manufactured, requiring more natural resources, and in most cases, we can save money. Conserving energy and natural resources is another way that we can make a difference. By turning off the lights when we leave a room or the water when we are not using it, or turning down the thermostat in our homes, all of these are small examples with huge impact potential. These are just a few examples of ways the individual can make a difference.

O – Opinion - Yes, I do believe that individuals can have a positive impact on the environment.

When you are stating the answer, you do not have to make it a formal statement by saying the word "opinion" at the beginning and end, but it does help to reinforce that it is your opinion of the question.

As I mentioned before, one prevalent place for impromptu questions is during a job interview. To better prepare yourself, there are many places on the internet or in books that you can get lists of possible questions to help you be better prepared, but it is virtually impossible to be prepared for every question. Some of the questions you hear make perfectly good sense as part of an interview and can be anticipated, for example, "What attracted you to this company? Tell us about your strengths. List five words that describe your character. Tell us about a time when you faced a challenge and how you overcame the challenge."

There are other times when the question seems rather strange or downright outlandish and you may have no idea what to say. Your first thought may be to wonder what in the world the question has to do with the job for which you are interviewing. In some instances, the question may be asked to gauge your thought process, or how you handle yourself when challenged. Some examples of this type of question may be, "Why is there fuzz on a tennis ball? Can you name at least 10 other uses for a pencil besides writing? If you could be any color crayon, which color would you be and why? What cartoon character would best describe you?" Yes, these are *actual questions* taken from lists of potential interview questions.

For the second example of the Speech Cookie OREO Method, let's look at one of these questions and a possible response. (I personally know at least two people who have been asked this question in an interview.)

Question: If you could be any fruit or vegetable, what would you be and why?

After you get over the initial shock of the question, just think of the Speech Cookie OREO Method and your response may be something like this:

O – **Opinion** - I believe that if I could be any fruit or vegetable, I would be a fresh stalk of celery.

R – **Reason(s)** – When you think about a fresh stalk of celery, it is crisp and a beautiful fresh shade of green with little leaves that resemble funny looking hair on the top. This reminds me that sometimes we have to play life straight and deal with serious situations, but the leafy "hair" reminds me to have fun, don't take myself too seriously and enjoy life.

E – Example(s) – An example of this attitude from my life is when I am working in a team. We usually have a goal to achieve or a task to complete which may be serious, but research shows that the more people "play" together with a positive attitude, the level of stress is greatly reduced, which leads to greater production and more cohesiveness in the team.

O – Opinion – That's why when I am asked what fruit or vegetable I would be if I had to choose, a nice fresh stalk of celery comes to mind.

Obviously, there are many fruits or vegetables one could choose from to respond to this question, but you can see how it can work within the framework of the Speech Cookie OREO Method.

As we discussed, an impromptu question can be asked in many situations. Some situations are simply casual conversation; others may be for the "crown" or for that opportunity of a lifetime. Whatever the circumstance, the next time you are asked a question, think of the simple four step structure for greater success. Hmmmm, anyone else hungry for some cookies and milk?

Added Challenge: How would you respond to these two questions using the Speech Cookie OREO Method?

The terms Speech Cookie and Speech Cookie OREO Method are original copywritten terms by Tammy Miller and may only be used when giving full credit to the originator. Any questions, please contact the author.

Speech Cookie: Think of a time when you were asked a question that completely stumped you or caught you off guard and how you might use the Speech Cookie OREO Method to provide a better response. Or, think of a couple of questions that you might hear in an interview or work place meeting and use the Speech Cookie OREO Method to develop possible responses.

1. Question: _____

       O: _____

       R: _____

       E: _____

       O: _____

2. Question: _____

       O: _____

       R: _____

       E: _____

       O: _____

3. Question: _____

       O: _____

       R: _____

       E: _____

       O: _____

Notes and Key Points From This Chapter:

_____

_____

_____

_____

_____

_____

_____

_____

_____

_____

_____

_____

_____

_____

_____

_____

Chapter Three
(Of Course!)
Think in Threes

There are several "structures" we can use in putting a presentation together, and we look at many of these in the coming chapters. However, I would like to offer a quick glimpse at a proven structure, to get you thinking in a way that may be an entirely new thought process.

A fundamental concept throughout this book is to always start by "**Thinking in Threes**" when looking for material, or perhaps it could be stated to think of *at least three things* you could talk about with every topic. You will quickly recognize this method in the coming chapters as we look at where we find material all around us. It may seem like a simple concept, but when you fully engage in this process, you will find it will not only help build your creativity in speaking and writing, but also in other communication exchanges, and it can be FUN.

It is thought that the human mind can most easily recall three to five points when they hear someone speak or are trying to recall details. With this in mind, when we are putting presentations together a great place to start is by thinking of at least three points you could use for your presentation.

In the same manner that our Speech Cookie© helped provide a structure for impromptu speaking, a quick glimpse at a proven structure for presenting is to use:

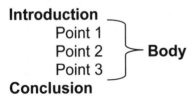

Introduction
     Point 1
     Point 2   **Body**
     Point 3
Conclusion

This is a very basic structure that can be used for almost any type of a presentation, including when you are **informing, persuading, motivating, inspiring or entertaining**. (The different types are explained in greater detail in the next chapter.) In Chapter Sixteen we look at this structure in much greater detail, but the main idea for this chapter is to get you **thinking in threes**, or again, at least three things you could talk about with any given topic.

The number three, itself, can act as a visual reminder for the more visual people reading this book. The first loop represents the **Introduction**; the center represents the **Body**; and the bottom loop is the **Conclusion**:

Introduction

Body (3 points)

Conclusion

Thinking in Threes

I mentioned that this concept can be FUN, and those who know me know I love to have fun. The idea is to look at ANY item that you see in front of you and think of at least three things you could talk about. As you get started, don't worry about the purpose of your presentation, but just start by **thinking in threes**.

Thinking in Threes: For this chapter exercise, choose at least *eight* words and think of at least three things you could talk about with each word. This may be a new concept, so if this doesn't come very easily, don't worry, there will be plenty of opportunities to build this skill throughout the book.

Word 1: _____

       Talking points: _____

Word 2: _____

       Talking points: _____

Word 3: _____

       Talking points: _____

Word 4: _____

       Talking points: _____

Word 5: _____

       Talking points: _____

Word 6: _____

       Talking points: _____

Word 7: _____

       Talking points: _____

Word 8: _____

       Talking points: _____

Notes and Key Points From This Chapter:

_____

_____

_____

_____

_____

_____

_____

_____

_____

_____

_____

_____

_____

_____

_____

Chapter Four
Purposeful Presenting

Audience Analysis and Adaptation

We cannot talk about purposeful presenting without briefly discussing audience analysis. As you are thinking about the purpose of the presentation you also have to ask yourself the questions, "Who is my audience and what are they expecting?" As a speaker, you must have a good understanding of this concept as you are putting your presentation together. For example, if you are talking about the importance of emergency first aid, how would the presentation differ if you were addressing your co-workers; your seven year old nephew; or a community group who you were asking to provide the funding so you could teach classes related to this topic? Each audience has a different expectation, and your presentation would need to be different in structure and wording for these different audiences.

There are several factors to consider in regards to audience analysis:
1. What is my audience expecting?
2. What do they already know about the topic?
3. How is the audience going to use your information?
4. What do you have in common with your audience?
5. Are demographics an issue (age, race, religion, location of audience, background, etc.)?
6. If this is a persuasive presentation, how do they already feel about the topic?
7. If you are persuading the audience, are there key points that you know they are against and what are you using to alleviate these concerns?

You may be asking yourself how to get this information. How you get the information will vary depending on the audience and topic. In some cases, you can just ask ahead of time. You can ask the person or people who have asked you to speak. You can look at the demographics for the area, provided by public information. You can test your information on similar groups. These are just a few of the ways you can glean this information, just keep in mind that **the more you know about your audience, the better your message can be adapted to the purpose**.

Types of Presentations

There are several different types of presentations that you can use to convey your message. The type can vary depending on how you interpret the presentation. These can include informing, persuading, motivating, inspiring, entertaining, instructional, farewell, commemorative, roast or toast, retirement, and many other categories.

One reason that there are so many interpretations is that some presentations have elements of multiple types combined. For example, you can inform an audience and you can persuade an audience; you can inform but not persuade; but it is very difficult to persuade an audience without some element of informing. Or, you can motivate and inspire, or inspire and persuade, or entertain and roast, just to give a few examples.

Sometimes the *situation* determines the type. Sometimes the *subject matter* determines the type. Sometimes the *person* determines the type. Sometimes the type is determined by the *location*. There are a lot of factors, and yes, it can be confusing, so let's go back to the basic question, **"What do you want your audience to understand, feel, or do when they leave your presentation?"**

Asking this question while you are assembling your presentation will help guide you with, not only a structure but the language that you will use. **The type of presentation may vary but the question that helps direct you will**

remain the same. To better understand this, we need to better understand the basic differences between the types of presentations.

Informing: When the purpose is to inform your audience, the key element is to convey information. You are usually presenting just the facts. The presentation is generally more objective and you are looking at *knowledge* instead of emotion in conveying the message to your audience. Your goal is to give the audience more information than they had before listening to your presentation.

A large majority of the presentations you give or hear fall under the category of informing. You might be giving someone new information or telling/showing them how something works. You could be talking about people, or animals, or events, or concepts, just to name a few. The foundation for informing is to convey information.

It is amazing to me how many people think they do not have anything to share of interest to others. When I have asked a few of these people what they do, I get all kinds of valuable answers including computer technology, taking minutes in meetings, doing massage therapy, and the list goes on and on. Just from this brief list there are some wonderful presentations that could inform an audience. I don't know about you, but with technology changing by the nanosecond, I would love to hear an informative presentation about computer technology,(especially if they can help me decipher all of these social networks out there), or how to take effective meeting minutes, or some quick tips on how I can relive stress with massage therapy – very valuable presentations. Don't ever underestimate the vast array of information you can present to an audience.

Persuading: When you are persuading your audience, you are asking them to involve *emotion, human need, behavior values* or *policy*. You may be asking them to agree with what you are stating, or take what you are stating and disagree. In contrast to just informing your audiences, when you are persuading you are often presenting the facts, then telling your audience how they should feel about, or use the facts you are presenting. Persuasive techniques are more geared toward subjective behavior, and you may want your audience to change their thoughts or behavior related to your topic.

When addressing values, it is helpful to know, "Why does your audience feel the way they do?" The more you know about your audience, the more effective you will be in persuading them to agree or disagree with your stand on an issue. For example, if you are presenting a difficult or controversial topic and you know your audience is against what you are presenting, the more research you do on *why* your audience feels this way, the better chance you will have in helping them understand that there may be different ways to look at the topic.

In many controversial situations, the bottom line is the lack of a clear understanding of the topic, or not enough information. Maybe there is misinformation involved that you can help make clearer (this is an example of the "inform to persuade" concept).

Policy is another area where the ability to persuade an audience can play a key role. With policy, it may be imperative to explain the policy in detail first, to make sure you and the members of the audience are at the same starting point with the facts, and then move into changing the policy.

One element of persuasive presenting that is often overlooked is the *call to action*. If your goal is to get your audience to take action and support a cause or make a change, don't forget to *ask them* to do just that. For example, if you want someone to write to a political figure to make a statement for or against a topic, tell your audience the action you want them to take AND, give them the names and addresses of who to contact to take this action. If you want someone to sign a petition, provide the petition for them to sign. Too often, a presenter will tell an audience they want them to take an action but do not provide the tools to take the next step.

When you are persuading an audience, you also have a choice about persuading them to SUPPORT your ideas or be AGAINST what you are presenting. There are many references out there to help you use persuasive language, and here is a quick list of words for persuasion to give you a better understanding of the power of persuasive words:

Support: Advantages; expectation; most important; strongly recommend; and support

Against: Against; damaging; disadvantages; harmful; and terrible

Persuasion is all around us, no matter where we live or what we do. If there is contact with another person or media, on any level, there can be persuasion. Think about the advertising methods that surround you daily, or how you get your children or employees to do something. Persuasion can be obvious or subtle, but it almost always involves our emotions, human needs, behaviors, values or policy issues.

Motivating: When you are motivating an audience, there will certainly be elements of persuasion involved, but the tone is often softer and the language less forceful. Motivational presentations are often *goal driven* whereby you are asking your audience to set a goal, personal or professional, and put the steps in action to achieve the desired goal. The key to motivating in a presentation is helping the audience understand *why* they are doing something, or why they should do something. If they do not know the reasons, you can help them understand the reason for their actions. Did you note the word, *should*? This is another example of the blending of presentation types. The word "should" indicates that you may be motivating and persuading. The difference can be subtle and is often determined by your tone.

Inspiring: Like motivating, an inspiring presentation can have elements of persuasion. The differences between motivating an audience and inspiring them can again be very subtle. Instead of the idea of logic to motivate, the inspiring presentation deals more with the listener's emotions. You are often asking the audience to seek a higher emotional level. Sometimes, you are sharing stories of challenges and hardships, and how these were overcome by you or someone else. You are appealing to the common bond of humanity and heart and asking the audience to take this information and walk away wanting to be a better person because they heard what you were presenting.

Entertaining: When entertaining an audience it is for pure pleasure. You are not in front of the group to make them think, but just to allow them to enjoy the whole experience.

There is also a misconception that entertaining presentations always have to be funny. This is not the case. Entertainment and humor can be closely related, and many entertaining presentations are funny, or have elements of humor, but the foundation of an entertaining presentation is to provide pleasure for your audience.

Hopefully, in reading over these distinctions you have a better understanding of the fundamental differences of the speech types. Clearly, there are presentations that span more than one type, and sometimes the differences are very subtle, so therefore, we go back to the basic question…

"What do I want my audience to understand, feel, or do when they leave my presentation?"

Specific Message

When you are developing a presentation, it is imperative to decide what your "specific message" is going to be as you are preparing the information. People refer to this message by different names, including residual message, statement of purpose, main strategy, or purpose statement, but essentially, you are asking yourself the question, **"What do I want my audience to understand, feel, or do when they leave my presentation?"** The response to this question should be as simple as one sentence, because it is the *specific message* of your presentation and will direct your structure, language, and focus. This sentence generally contains your main points as this makes us the pieces of what you are going to say to convey your message.

To examine this on the most basic level, let's look at informing vs. persuading. As a student and teacher of communication experiences for many years, I have heard many wonderful presentations. These have included topics that were creative, awe-inspiring, persuasive, and thought provoking presentations.

One memorable presentation involved a demonstration on how to make a peanut butter and jelly sandwich. In fact, my mother can give several presentations relating to travel experiences, but a common theme for her would be her philosophy that she can travel anywhere and survive, as long as she has a jar of peanut butter and a box of granola bars.

Throughout the book we look at a multitude of ways to generate topics and points, so for this example, let's choose Peanut Butter as the topic.

If the main focus in to *inform* the audience and we ask, **"What do I want my audience to understand, feel, or do when they leave my presentation?"** a sample of the responses and some possible points could be:

Specific Message: I want my audience to gain basic information about peanut butter including the first known use of peanut butter; how peanut butter is made; and where most peanut butter comes from.

      Point 1: The first known use of peanut butter
      Point 2: How peanut butter is made
      Point 3: Where most peanut butter comes from

OR…

Specific Message: I want my audience to have some great peanut butter recipes, including kiss cookies; peanut butter pie; and peanut butter and tomato soup.

      Point 1: How peanut butter kiss cookies are made
      Point 2: The making of chocolate peanut butter pie
      Point 3: Making peanut butter and tomato soup
      (honest, this is a real recipe).

You can see the difference between the *specific message* and the main points. The purpose is the overall answer to the statement, **"What I want my audience to understand, feel or do when they leave the presentation"**.

This list looks like we are simply informing the audience, however, if we expand each one a little further, it sounds much more like persuasion:

Specific Message: I want my audience to understand the value of peanut butter, including how it has changed our culture; how easy it is to make healthy snacks; and why our diets would be much healthier if we added peanut butter.

1. To gain basic information about peanut butter and understand why it has changed our culture for the better.
2. To get some great recipe ideas and understand that it doesn't take a lot of effort to make healthy snacks with peanut butter.

3. To learn the nutritional facts about peanut butter and understand that if we add more peanut butter to our diet, we will be much healthier.

You can "hear" the difference between informing and persuading by simply adding a few choice words to the point. With the second set of points, each point is using persuasive language, including, "changed for the better"; "healthy snacks"; and "healthier". By adding these few words, you get the sense that the speaker is trying to persuade the audience that peanut butter is a good food, not just inform the audience about peanut butter. Yet, the speaker is informing the audience to persuade them. This is just a quick example of informing vs. persuading your audience.

Disclaimer: If you do not believe that peanut butter is a healthy food, please do not contact me with angry messages – this is just to prove a point about informing and persuading in a presentation. ☺

When we are looking at the various ways to develop points for your presentation throughout the book, always keep in mind your basic question: **"What do I want my audience to understand, feel, or do when they leave my presentation?"**

To narrow down the wide variety of types of presentations you can give, we will focus primarily on the following five types of presentations in this book:

1. Informing
2. Persuading
3. Motivating
4. Inspiring
5. Entertaining

With many topics, you will recognize that by changing the language you use in your presentation, the topic can be tailored to fit a variety of purposes, as noted in the peanut butter example where the topic is the same, but the specific message is different.

The exercise for this chapter is to think of **three** topics (imagine that!), then think of **three** different purposes for the presentation (informative, persuasive, motivating, entertaining or inspiring), and **three** things you could talk about with each presentation type.

This is an extremely important concept so let's look at an example of how this might work.

The topic for this example is **KEYS**

Informative presentation using **KEYS**:
    1. History of making keys
    2. How keys are made
    3. How to re-key a lock

Entertaining presentation using **KEYS**:
    1. The time I lost my keys at the lake
    2. The last time I locked my keys in the car
    3. Setting off the car alarm three times in one day

Motivating presentation using **KEYS**:
    1. To believe in yourself is a key to success
    2. Education is a key to success
    3. Attitude is a key to success

Your first thoughts may have been of car or house keys, but you could have also thought of keys to success, Florida Keys, the key to my heart, an acronym for safe hiking (KEYS to Hiking Safety – **K** – Keep in touch, **E** – Ever watchful of dangers on the trail, **Y** – Your location – always know where you are, and **S** – Stay with Others – never hike alone.) This was a BONUS for you – acronyms as points. There are many "key" thoughts (I love puns!) you could have with this topic. You are truly only limited by your imagination – a "key" to **thinking in threes**.

Topic 1: _____

Type of Presentation: _____

Specific Message: _____

_____

     Point 1: _____

     Point 2: _____

     Point 3: _____

Type of Presentation: _____

Specific Message: _____

_____

     Point 1: _____

     Point 2: _____

     Point 3: _____

Type of Presentation: _____

Specific Message: _____

_____

     Point 1: _____

     Point 2: _____

     Point 3: _____

Topic 2: _____

Type of Presentation: _____

Specific Message: _____

_____

Point 1: _____

Point 2: _____

Point 3: _____

Type of Presentation: _____

Specific Message: _____

_____

Point 1: _____

Point 2: _____

Point 3: _____

Type of Presentation: _____

Specific Message: _____

_____

Point 1: _____

Point 2: _____

Point 3: _____

Topic 3: _____

Type of Presentation: _____

Specific Message: _____

_____

      Point 1: _____

      Point 2: _____

      Point 3: _____

Type of Presentation: _____

Specific Message: _____

_____

      Point 1: _____

      Point 2: _____

      Point 3: _____

Type of Presentation: _____

Specific Message: _____

_____

      Point 1: _____

      Point 2: _____

      Point 3: _____

Notes and Key Points From This Chapter:

_____

_____

_____

_____

_____

_____

_____

_____

_____

_____

_____

_____

_____

_____

_____

_____

_____

_____

Chapter Five
Success in Life

We started this book by looking at real life situations and how we can take these situations and develop them into effective, valuable presentations. Every person has real life experiences to draw from, some happy, some not as happy, but all filled with lessons learned, challenges met, or great stories to share. Look inside, look in the mirror, and look around you – these treasures are everywhere.

We are often inspired by "success" stories we hear about the lives of other people, but many of us can share stories of our own lives and the different levels of success in varying areas that can inspire others. Lance Miller, 2005 World Champion of Public Speaking, states, *"In order to inspire an audience, we must learn for ourselves how to live an inspired life."* The information in this chapter helps us realize that the word "success" can be very subjective and can have multiple meanings. It is a true statement that success is not just about money and fame.

Begin With Yourself

If you are old enough to be reading this information, you are old enough to have a ton of information that you could present, that people around you would find valuable. The idea of "valuable" to some people is a little intimidating. Often I hear people state, "I don't have anything to say that anyone else would like to hear".

If you are a human being, then your life situations have probably been experienced by others. (If you are not a human being, then there is a ton of information you can share with your audience on extraterrestrial living, space travel, etc. – astronomical possibilities! ☺)

Other people can give a presentation on the same topic, but NO ONE can tell your story like you can. Your story doesn't have to be sensational, just sincere.

Using Your Successes

Even though our world in inundated with motivational speakers and materials, there are some people who believe they have never had successes or have been a success at anything in their life – shocking, I know. A few years ago my beautiful daughters bought me a lapel pin that states, "I am NOT a nag, I am a motivational speaker". I think they were trying to tell me something.

What about the successes you have had in your life? Even though I may not know you, I know I could name at least 10 accomplishments that most people have experienced in their life, providing there weren't any physical or mental challenges. For example, if you are reading this book, then you have successfully learned how to read. You most likely learned how to walk, talk (sometimes your family and friends may wish you weren't so successful, as you talk non-stop), say the alphabet, completed at least a few years of school, learned how to spell and write your name, learned to feed yourself and take a drink, and talk on the telephone.

These are elementary successes for most of us, and you may not think they could make an interesting presentation, but used as a foundation for a topic I see the list as follows:

Success & Possible Presentations

1. Read
   Literacy; Education in School; and Speed Reading

2. Walk
   Walking as Exercise, Charitable Walks; and The Passion for Walking Trails

3. Talk
       Toastmasters (of course.); Using Different Speech Structures; and How Words are Formed

4. Say the Alphabet
       Origins of the Alphabet; How the Alphabet Differs in Other Languages; and The History of the Alphabet Song

5. Completed at least a few years of school
       Educational Systems Throughout Your Own Country; Educational Systems Throughout the World; and The Value of a Higher Education

6. Learned how to spell your name
       Baby Names; What Your Name Means; and Child Development

7. Learned how to write your name
       Different Types of Fonts; Writing Analysis; and Why Some People Print and Others Use Cursive (where did that word come from anyway – hmmm, another topic)

8. Learned to feed yourself
       World Hunger; Hunger in Your Own Country; and Rotary International's Million Meals

9. Take a drink
       Alcoholic vs. Non-alcoholic Beverages; The Importance of Water to the Human Body; and Living with Lactose Intolerance

10. Talk on the telephone
       The History of the Telephone; Telephones and Technology; and Tin Can Telephones and Other Children's Games

Yes, that is right – the above list gives you 30 more presentation topics (actually 31 if you count cursive). You don't have to know everything (or anything, for that matter) about these topics, just something to consider, do some research, and put together a great presentation.

The word "success", in and of itself can make a great presentation. How do you define success? What does success mean to you? How can you tell if you have achieved success? How people achieve success is very important to others. If you want to be a speaker, you most likely listen to other speakers to see how they do it. You emulate what you like about what they do, and learn what not to do by observing what you didn't like. If you want to be an author, you may read a lot to see what works and doesn't work. If you want to learn another language, you find someone who can teach you the desired language. All of these are ways of looking at the value of success.

In today's society we hear a lot about coaching and mentoring. Coaching used to be a word we only heard on the athletic field, but now we learn from the success of others by engaging a life coach, or a speech coach. Or, perhaps, we coach others in various fields because we are good at what we do and want to share our expertise with others. As mentors, we help others determine what they are looking for on the job or in life and by working closely with them, we help them achieve their goals. What is the difference between coaching and mentoring? A great topic – look it up and share your knowledge in a presentation.

There are countless stories out there about people who have achieved success, from the not so famous to the famous. A few I can think of include stories about starting with very humble means and working to take that poor beginning to great success in business or industry. Or, dropping out of school to help support a family, and using this hard work ethic to achieve greatness. Or, being a single parent and raising two beautiful children that make you so proud every step of the way. True success does not have to include Hollywood and a lot of money, yes, sometimes those are the stories we hear most often, but true success can be very quiet and unassuming, depending on how one defines success.

Successes I Have Had in My Life: What successes have you had in your life that could be the foundation for a presentation? Below please list some successes you have had (remember, be creative) and at least three things you could talk about with each success.

1. _____

      Point 1: _____

      Point 2: _____

      Point 3: _____

2. _____

      Point 1: _____

      Point 2: _____

      Point 3: _____

3. _____

      Point 1: _____

      Point 2: _____

      Point 3: _____

4. _____

      Point 1: _____

      Point 2: _____

      Point 3: _____

Notes and Key Points From This Chapter:

_____

_____

_____

_____

_____

_____

_____

_____

_____

_____

_____

_____

_____

_____

_____

Chapter Six
Sharing Challenges

In many cases, the bond between you and your audience is the fact that you share something in common. A few years ago I had the opportunity to speak with many people in the workplace, one on one. Here is a story that began with two women. In talking with one woman, I found she had a son in high school and she was dealing with some challenges with her son. She felt like she was the only one dealing with this type of challenge. Another woman I spoke to, who did not know the first woman, even though they worked in the same building, had a very similar situation and she felt like she was the only one who was dealing with the situation.

The common bond was the situation, and when these two women realized that there were others out there who would understand and share the experience, the situation became much more bearable for both of them. In this case, I happened to be in the position to listen to both of their stories, and then introduced them to each other. In fact, a group of eight of us started a sharing group, calling ourselves, *Empowering Women*, to help each other understand that although we all face challenges, some of them are similar and some of them are different. When we started to share the challenges, and hopes and joys with each other, we were all able to come our stronger.

I am a firm believer that we do not know what we are being prepared for! Overcoming challenges is one of the great presentation topics. We all love to hear how the "underdog" persevered to overcome the sometimes unthinkable challenge. I know a woman, Karen, who lost her mother at the age of seven, her father remarried to an alcoholic who was abusive, she was raised by friends of her mother, her father was later arrested for murder, her husband was tragically killed in a construction accident, with two small children at home, and she was down sized from her job three times. She has overcome enormous challenges that sound more like a soap opera, or a country music song. Can you guess what she speaks about? It is hope! If there was ever an opportunity to give negative presentations, she may have it, but in her case, her faith has taught her to find the hope in all situations.

Another story related to challenges in life is one area where I get especially "jazzed"! "Jazzed" is my descriptive word for something I love to do and could do it all day. I am a cancer survivor, as you may have read in the bio, and I love to talk with other cancer patients, especially those who are newly diagnosed. I especially love to show how humor can be used in many situations that some people consider very serious, like a cancer diagnosis. There was nothing funny about being told I had cancer at the age of 42, that is for sure, but I COULD NOT CHANGE THE DIAGNOSIS. What I did have control over was my attitude. In my book, *The Lighter Side of Breast Cancer Recovery: Lessons Learned Along the Path to Healing*, I look at a very serious situation in a lighthearted manner. From crazy send off parties going into the hospital to clown noses and kazoos in the operating room, to crazy songs, and everything in between.

The presentations I have developed from this experience have dealt with laughter, humor, dealing with challenges, and offering hope, just to name a few. The correlation between the challenge and the presentations may be obvious, but one of the less obvious factors have been the many people who have heard my presentation or have seen me jumping and bouncing around on stage eight years after the diagnosis and seeing hope (these are not my words, but what others have told me). Perhaps it is hope for their future. Or in some cases, I have been told it is the first time they have laughed since the diagnosis.

If I had not faced this challenge, I would not have this important message to share with others. Again, *I am a firm believer that we do not know what we are being*

prepared for! If I had not built my communication skills, I would not be able to present a message that may make a difference in the lives of others. Craig Valentine, 1999 World Champion of Public Speaking, often says, "Don't get ready, stay ready". You just never know...

Most of us can think of people we know who have had life changing situations, sometimes wonderful and sometimes tales of true hardship. People who use these situations to help motivate or inspire can make such a difference in the lives of others. Sometimes the communication is done one on one, and other situations allow the communication to be presented to groups of people, from small groups to thousands of people at one time.

The final story of using challenges for this chapter involves a wonderful, inspiring young couple; Jamey and Molly (see the Resource Section for contact information). I had the honor of hearing their presentation recently, and it is a perfect example of people who use life changing events to help others. Their story is for them to tell, so I will just present the highlights here.

Jamey talks of an ordinary day in their lives. Molly felt tired and run down, but so might be the ordinary life of a first grade teacher like Molly. What they did not know was that Molly was suffering from streptococcus that very quickly turned to deadly sepsis. Within hours Molly was fighting for her life and the doctors gave her a 5% chance of survival.

The heart-wrenching story is one of love, dedication, inspiration, communication, decision making, the power of prayer, and the love of people. To save her life, Molly had to have her legs and some fingers amputated. Their lives were forever altered. There is no way that words on this page can convey all of the emotions in the presentation.

At the end of the presentation, as Molly walked to the stage, through the standing ovation of the audience to join her husband, I can guarantee you there was not a single dry eye in the room.

Now, Jamey and Molly take this inspirational story to audiences to help others understand their *Steps to Hope*. Their powerful message will continue to inspire audiences wherever they go. Since all of this happened in 2008, they are still working on this presentation to bring the best message to their audience, and are looking for places to speak about their experience.

The story of Molly and Jamey is truly inspirational at the very core and could be given as just that – an incredibly inspirational story. At some point they may choose to add additional elements to help their audience reflect on their own lives or maybe focus on certain aspects of the story, for example the communication with health care providers, or the experience with physical therapy. What they say and how they say it will depend greatly on the audience to whom they are speaking.

There are many ways they can present their incredible story. For the purpose of this book, and to use this as an example for putting a presentation together, let's focus on one possible structure idea they may use.

Since the word "steps" is such an integral part of the story, they may consider using their phrase, Steps to Hope, and use STEPS as an acronym for their message. For example, it could stand for:

Slow Down and Enjoy the Moment

Things to be Thankful for or Take Time to Reflect

Embrace Each Moment or Each Day is a Gift

Perseverance or Power of Prayer or Practicing Patience

Success Comes in Steps

There are many options available and I know that however Jamey and Molly decide to put their story together, I am sure it will impact the lives of many.

(Just before this book went to print, Jamey excitedly told me that both he and Molly became certified peer visitors for new amputees through the Amputee Coalition of America. You only have to meet this couple briefly to know what a tremendous impact they will have on the lives of the people they will talk with through this organization. The ability to help others understand the value of communication and attitude will be incredible. I will say it again; I am a firm believer that you just never know what you are being prepared for.)

You may have no idea how valuable your message about challenges you have faced, how you have faced them, and the ultimate outcome, could be to others as they see you and hear your message. It does not have to be a life threatening illness to make an impact – it just has to come from your heart and experience to make a difference.

Challenges I Have Faced

What challenges have you, or someone you know faced in your life that could be the foundation for a presentation? Below please list some challenges and at least three things you could talk about with each challenge.

1. _____

    Point 1: _____

    Point 2: _____

    Point 3: _____

2. _____

    Point 1: _____

    Point 2: _____

    Point 3: _____

3. _____

    Point 1: _____

    Point 2: _____

    Point 3: _____

4. _____

    Point 1: _____

    Point 2: _____

    Point 3: _____

Notes and Key Points From This Chapter:

_____

_____

_____

_____

_____

_____

_____

_____

_____

_____

_____

_____

_____

_____

_____

_____

Chapter Seven
Lessons Along the Journey of Life

Life is about the journey and not as much the destination. We may have heard the quote, in one variety or another, but when we are looking at presentation topics, the lessons we have learned along the journey of life offers us endless possibilities.

Let's start with an example of a friend, Mike, who runs a lot of marathons. He discovered, after running 22 marathons, that he just wasn't reaching his desired finish time. He hired a coach to find out how he could improve. The coach told him he had all the *tactics* in place to win, but he wasn't using the right *strategy*. He could easily give a presentation to fellow runners, or people interested in running about this experience and process, but he took it one step further. He realized that using the proper strategy in running a marathon was closely related to using the proper strategy in running his business. Using what he learned from the marathon coach, and applying this to his business, he has grown his business by more than 70%. Now, he can also talk to small business owners about using the right strategy to grow their business. He has taken a real life experience, realized the lesson and presents this lesson to others.

When I was going through cancer treatments, I needed to feel like I had control over some part of my life. To help keep my mind focused, I thought about what was happening as a journey. The structure I used to help focus the thinking was to develop 20 "lessons" I learned along the path to healing. In this case, the lessons served as the structure for my presentations. Depending on the time, audience and event, I can pick and choose the lessons I want to emphasize the most to highlight my points. Here are the lessons:

Lesson One – Don't put off your yearly exams. Make the call – schedule the appointment.

Lesson Two – Trust your own instincts.

Lesson Three – Keep a record of everything that is happening.

Lesson Four – Develop a personal mantra to replace negative thoughts.

Lesson Five – Recruit your personal Humor Team. (No cost involved.)

Lesson Six – Be prepared to put up your own personal shield of protection.

Lesson Seven – Start and keep a "Recovery File".

Lesson Eight – Find love and laughter everywhere.

Lesson Nine –Tell your closest family and friends of your diagnosis in person.

Lesson Ten – Be informed.

Lesson Eleven – Remain positive in every single way that you can – no matter how small.

Lesson Twelve - Write down the questions that you want to ask.

Lesson Thirteen – Look for the smallest blessings in each day.

Lesson Fourteen – Know that you have choices.

Lesson Fifteen – Remember, you are a unique person!

Lesson Sixteen – Celebrate the smallest victories.

Lesson Seventeen – Accept that there are some things in life we cannot change.

Lesson Eighteen – Keep your doctors and health care providers accountable.

Lesson Nineteen – Thank your healthcare providers.

Lesson Twenty – Live life to the fullest!

From each of these twenty lessons, I could develop an entire presentation by using some of the elements we have discussed. For example, *Lesson One - Don't put off your yearly exams. Make the call – schedule the appointment.* If I was thinking of three points related just to this topic I could use:
        1. Recommended Exams at Certain Ages
        2. The Value of Early Detection in Cancer Treatment
        3. Uninsured? Where to Get Free Exams

Or, *Lesson Eight - Find love and laughter everywhere.*
        1. The Healing Value of Humor
        2. What Makes People Laugh
        3. Different Levels of Love

In fact, each of these points could be another presentation. See how this work? You are really only limited by your imagination.

The lessons can be very straightforward, such as, *I burned myself on the kitchen stove,* and turn this lesson into a presentation on home safety. It does not have to be a long drawn out experience to make an effective presentation and valuable lesson.

Lessons I Have Learned Along My Journey Called Life

You may have similar experiences where you learned a valuable lesson along your path and can share this knowledge with someone else. Lessons can be from your childhood, home life, workplace, community service, raising children, dealing with a divorce or illness, caring for an elderly parent and the list goes on and on.

What lessons have you learned along your journey called life that could be the foundation for a presentation? Below please list some lessons you have learned and at least three things you could talk about with each lesson.

1. _____

       Point 1: _____

       Point 2: _____

       Point 3: _____

2. _____

       Point 1: _____

       Point 2: _____

       Point 3: _____

3. _____

       Point 1: _____

       Point 2: _____

       Point 3: _____

Notes and Key Points From This Chapter:

_____

_____

_____

_____

_____

_____

_____

_____

_____

_____

_____

_____

_____

_____

_____

_____

_____

Chapter Eight
People I Have Met

When you first read this topic, you may have thought that you haven't met anyone famous that anyone else would like to hear about. Like the word success, "famous" can be very subjective.

I have had a true honor and privilege to meet and talk with country music legend, Dolly Parton, on a couple of occasions. I can go on record right here and tell you that I believe she is a living angel and there is almost a glow around the woman when you meet her. From this experience, I have given many presentations about Dolly and her life from very humble beginnings to great success in the music industry. Indeed, many would consider her a famous person and may want to hear about my experience meeting her. She has also inspired me in many ways, and her songs have inspired some of my presentations, but more on that later in the book.

Dolly may be considered a famous person, but there are people around us everyday who inspire us and provide a solid foundation for a fantastic presentation. For me, it would include my incredible mother, my beautiful daughters, my other family members, and many friends who have inspired me in some way to share a message with others. Presentation topics from these people include living life from humble beginnings, dealing with adversity, caring for elderly parents, the joy of photography, the love and innocence of children, and on and on.

Maybe you have met someone from your community who is working to help change lives, or make life better for someone they may or may not know. It could be that you inspire others through your charitable work, or how you overcame a challenge in your life. Or, it could be that there is someone you would like to meet, or have studied in the past that you find fascinating for whatever reason. This category is *people you have met*, but it could just as easily extend to people you would like to have met before they passed on, or would like to meet in the future.

Most people like to hear about other people. They inspire us, motivate us, excite and thrill us by what they do and say, encourage us or inform us, but so many messages in presentations are about people. My life has been so blessed with people I have met along the way, and I am sure there are people in your life who have inspired you to help spread a message to others.

Through my speaking experiences and involvement with international organizations, I have been honored to meet people from around the world. I love to hear the stories from their countries, but what I have learned that I find most valuable is that no matter where we are from, no matter what our backgrounds, most people share common goals of peace, love, friendship, and happy lives filled with safety and joy. It seems as though the more people I meet from around the world, the more I realize we are similar in so many ways. This is a great presentation topic, and as we all know, our lives are just speech material!

Who have you met in your life that would make a good foundation for a presentation? Think about what it is about this person that stands out from others you have met and what you would like to say about this person.

Dolly Parton
and Tammy

People I Have Met

Below please list some of the people you have met and at least three things you could talk about with each person.

1. _____

      Point 1: _____

      Point 2: _____

      Point 3: _____

2. _____

      Point 1: _____

      Point 2: _____

      Point 3: _____

3. _____

      Point 1: _____

      Point 2: _____

      Point 3: _____

4. _____

      Point 1: _____

      Point 2: _____

      Point 3: _____

Notes and Key Points From This Chapter:

_____

_____

_____

_____

_____

_____

_____

_____

_____

_____

_____

_____

_____

_____

_____

Chapter Nine
Speechwriting – Dolly Style

From ABBA to ZZTop, your favorite songs can be an excellent springboard of information for your next presentation.

In a previous chapter, I mentioned meeting Dolly Parton and being inspired by her to give presentations on a variety of topics. Meeting Dolly is not the only way she has inspired my presentations. You may or may not know that Dolly has written over 3,000 songs over her career, starting when she was just a few years old. Many of her songs have been inspired by her real life experiences, just as many of our presentations are inspired by real life experiences (hmm, sounds like a great book title, My Life is Just Speech Material!).

Song Titles

Another great way to challenge yourself to develop presentation topics is to look at song titles and see how you could use just the title to inspire your presentations. You can certainly follow the same process with lyrics or sets of lyrics of your favorite songs, as we discuss later in this chapter. For example, it often amazes me how some songwriters seem to be writing songs about MY life. Perhaps this has happened to you, but let's starts with just the titles.

I do not have to look at Dolly's vast library of song titles to be able to choose a few that inspire presentations. Just a few of her most popular pieces can be effective. An example of this method of speech development would be:

Song Title: Working 9 to 5
> Employment Options; Office Life vs. Stay at Home Options; and Great Jobs That Make You Want to Go to Work

Song Title: I Will Always Love You
 Living with the Loss of a Loved One; The Bond
 Between a Mother and Daughter; and The Impact of a
 Challenged Child on Your Life

Song Title: Light of a Clear Blue Morning
 Overcoming Obstacles; Nighttime Safety; and The
 Affect of Sunlight on Our Mood

Song Title: The Grass is Blue
 Nursery Rhymes; Nonsensical Statements; and What
 Colors Mean to People

Song Title: Just Because I'm a Woman
 The Glass Ceiling in Business; Women in the
 Workplace; and The High Cost of Beauty

There you have it – 15 more presentation topics to consider.
This list was generated from some of her most popular
songs, and I could generate many more from other Dolly
Parton songs that may not be in the mainstream, for
example, "Silver and Gold", is a great title to give a
presentation on, The Currency Market; Silver and Gold
Jewelry, Which is Better Suited for Your Skin Tone; and
What Does it Take to Get A Gold Record? (That's a bonus
three more topics for you.)

These topics are generated without knowing the meaning or
story behind the song. If you have this added information,
you will surely have even more presentations from the song
titles.

Dolly is just one of my favorite music artists and I am sure I
could identify many more topics from her song titles, or the
titles of other singer/songwriters with whom I personally
identify, or when I simply hear an interesting song title.

Song Titles: Who do you identify with when it comes to song titles? On the following lines, identify your favorite singers/songwriters and a few song titles you can use. Then, identify at least three points you could make with each song title.

ARTIST # 1: _____

Song Title #1: _____

      Point 1: _____

      Point 2: _____

      Point 3: _____

Song Title #2:

      Point 1: _____

      Point 2: _____

      Point 3: _____

Song Title #3:

      Point 1: _____

      Point 2: _____

      Point 3: _____

ARTIST # 2: _____

Song Title #1: _____

      Point 1: _____

      Point 2: _____

Point 3: _____

Song Title #2:

    Point 1: _____

    Point 2: _____

    Point 3: _____

Song Title #3:

    Point 1: _____

    Point 2: _____

    Point 3: _____

ARTIST # 3: _____

Song Title #1: _____

    Point 1: _____

    Point 2: _____

    Point 3: _____

Song Title #2:

    Point 1: _____

    Point 2: _____

    Point 3: _____

Song Title #3:

        Point 1: _____

        Point 2: _____

        Point 3: _____

Added Challenge: For an added challenge, number a piece of paper from 1 – 20 and see if you can identify 20 different song titles that you could use as a foundation for a presentation. Then work on the points for each song title. This can also be a great icebreaker for a meeting, a topic for a group of friends, or at your next family event.

Song Lines

We started the chapter looking at song titles to develop presentations, now let's look at lyrics from songs, or "song lines".

In Dolly's song, Wildflowers, one line is, "Wildflowers Don't Care Where They Grow", is a great song line to inspire presentations on:

1. Daring to be Different
2. Traveling Along Life's Highway
3. Why Flowers Bring us Joy

Listening to the lyrics of songs can also inspire great presentations. The next time you hear some music, think of how you can take the song lines and turn them into the story line of your next presentation.

Notes and Key Points From This Chapter:

_____

_____

_____

_____

_____

_____

_____

_____

_____

_____

_____

_____

_____

_____

_____

_____

_____

Chapter Ten
Lessons From the Animal Kingdom

For anyone reading this book that has or has ever had pets, you probably can already think of a few examples of stories or lessons you have learned from your pets. If we take that one step further to include the animal kingdom, there are even more stories or lessons learned that we can relate with interest to an audience.

Let's begin the stories in this section with a turtle. A number of years ago my daughters gave me a gift of a tiny soft plastic turtle, we named Myrtle, to keep on my dash to remind me to slow down in life. It was a very sweet gesture and I loved to look at this little turtle when I was quickly heading off to my next meeting or appointment to remind me that life is way too short and slow down. I gave a presentation using my turtle as a visual aid to remind others about the pace of life – where it is and where it should be.

One bright, sunny day I was going around a corner with the window down – slowly (honest!) - and I watched in despair as my little Myrtle slid all the way across the dash to the other side of the vehicle and promptly flew out the window, just like she was trying to escape the confines of the vehicle to the great outdoors. I was at a very busy intersection and could not stop the vehicle to try and locate my precious gift. The following day, a Saturday, when I may have been able to retrieve my little reminder, it rained terribly and I wasn't able to send out a search party for Myrtle. I know my little Myrtle is probably, even today, floating somewhere under the roadways, or maybe has even escaped to the wide open ocean. Either way, although I do not have my precious Myrtle, I have purchased another turtle to be a constant reminder of the pace that one should go in life – slowly and savor every moment.

There are all kinds of lessons we can learn from our animals that can lead to great presentations. My youngest daughter, Lacey, has a reputation for "growing" very large cats! Her precious Tyke is 29 pounds and is 36 inches long. Yes, this is a domesticated housecat, not a mountain lion! I asked her what lessons she has learned from Tyke and she said, "That no matter how you look, someone will always love you and snuggle with you." Even at his size, he is still her "baby" and she loves him. I think this lesson has made her much more patient in life, especially in the wonderful work she does when working with children and animals.

My oldest daughter, Tiffany, has learned all kinds of lessons from her animals. From the tragic loss of her precious Maggie to the funny antics of her sweet Bailey, the lessons are plentiful. Her favorite animal lessons are…

Her sweet Maggie taught her the fine art of unconditional love - giving and receiving. She says, "Every day when I came home from work, I got 15 minutes of fame, as if it was the first time she'd seen me that day... every single day. No matter how bad a day, when I walked in that door and she jumped, yapped and wagged her entire body, I momentarily forgot about the angry client, the stacks of paperwork and the ringing phones. And I could never stay mad at her - the very few times she did something wrong. All it took was those big brown eyes and a sloppy kiss and I couldn't care about the mess in the next room."

Now she has a rambunctious kitten named Bailey who reminds her to laugh each and every day. About Bailey, she says, "When I least expect it, he's chasing bugs on the other side of the screen door, playing fetch with a piece of paper (yes, really!), and launching a sneak attack as I come around the corner - leaping over a foot in the air, straight up! Just as I start to get frustrated when he's chasing my hand while trying to make the bed, he stops and flops over, wanting a belly rub - how can I not laugh at that escape from trouble?"

My sweet Molly was my "Princess Cat" for almost 18 years – a very long time in cat years. Shortly before this book was published, we had to say good-bye to Molly, but over the years, her lessons were many. Each morning as I would leave the house, I would turn around and say, "I love you Molly", even if she was no where in sight. This always served as another reminder to me to tell those special people in my life how much I love them. Even now, I still take that extra moment to tell her as I walk out the door.

Another great cat story I have heard involved looking at daily life, in fact daily journal entries, from the cat's perspective. In this particular case it was how the cat was plotting revenge against her "person" for not feeding her the good food that the person enjoyed. It was very funny and thoroughly entertaining.

What lessons have the animals in your life taught you and what would you say about the lessons?

Nature is all around us, which means that speech material is all around us. I love to take nature pictures, especially of flowers and butterflies. If you haven't taken the time to really look at the wonder of creation around us, take a moment, put the book down, and go for a long nature walk. Not only will it relax you, but with your new passion for locating speech material, you will see the world in a whole new way. Or, better yet, take the book with you and use the notes section to record all the wonderful thoughts you have while on the nature trail.

My passion for butterflies has taken me to many beautiful locations to photograph their striking colors and the true gracefulness with which they glide through the air. I do not have fancy camera equipment, but I have been able to capture some of the most beautiful butterfly photos in butterfly parks and in nature. These photographs have provided a lot of speech material over the years.

You may or may not know this, but if you look at the back of the head of many butterfly species, you can actually see a smiley face. Really! Check it out, and if you can't see them, give me a call and I will share some photos with you.

With many animals, including the butterfly, sometimes the intention is for them to stand out in the world, and other times the idea is to hide from their predators by using their body parts, or wings in the case of the butterfly, as a natural camouflage. I have some incredible photos with the camouflaged wings hiding the butterfly as it sits clearly on a rock, but it is virtually impossible to see at quick glance.

On of my favorite presentations used various butterfly pictures to discuss how we get along with each other in the world. I used some photos of the beautiful, colorful butterflies to talk about how beautiful and unique we are as individuals. I used the camouflage butterflies to talk about how sometimes we need to have time for ourselves and "hide out" from the world, just to think about who we are and where we are going. I talked about butterflies on their own, and with other butterflies, with the idea that sometimes we need others to help us along the path. I finished with the smiley face butterfly to remind us of one of my philosophies and favorite quotes by an unknown author, "Sometimes the only sense we can make out of life is a sense of humor". This last point reflected on ways to find humor and smiles among all the situations and challenges that life can throw our way.

This is just a small example of using butterflies as a basis for a presentation, and how the presentation was enhanced by using the photographs to reinforce the points.

Another favorite use from the animal kingdom comes from just watching birds. I certainly do not consider myself a bird watcher, knowing the species, habitats, or migration paths, of birds, although this would make a great presentation. I do, however, love to just watch them and have been inspired by the graceful soaring of eagles overhead, the watchful eyes of the hawk, and the playfulness of little yellow finch, hmm, there are three points that would make a great speech.

One day I was watching a few birds, on a very windy day, as they were flying through the bright blue sky. What caught my attention on this day was the way they seemed to literally be playing in the wind. As I watched, they soared high then low and back up again. It truly looked as though they were just playing in the wind and with each other. When was the last time you just took a break and played? Oops, I better stop here before I get into another speech, but you get the idea.

Recently, I spoke at a conference at a beautiful resort in West Virginia. It was situated in the mountains and had a view out of the window of the lake and surrounding area that was just picturesque. Since it was elevated, and the large picture windows were nestled high above the lake, it looked like you were sitting in the clouds. I hadn't realized just how high we were until I noticed something out of the corner of my eye. It took me a few seconds to realize that there were several birds flying through the sky at eye level. The thought was instantly funny, but quickly leaped to "What type of speech could I do with this?" (Are you surprised??) Thinking in threes, as we are being taught to do, I thought...

> Topic 1: The Life of a Bird
> Topic 2: The Multitude of Birds in the World
> Topic 3: Red Skeleton and His Character, Heathcliff the Seagull.

The animal kingdom has so much material to offer speakers about life lessons. Take a moment and just watch the world around you and be inspired, then go out and inspire others.

Lessons From the Animal Kingdom: Below please list some of your observations from the animal kingdom, either in nature or closer to home, and three different presentations you could use from each observation.

1. _____

      Point 1: _____

      Point 2: _____

      Point 3: _____

2. _____

      Point 1: _____

      Point 2: _____

      Point 3: _____

3. _____

      Point 1: _____

      Point 2: _____

      Point 3: _____

4. _____

      Point 1: _____

      Point 2: _____

      Point 3: _____

Notes and Key Points From This Chapter:

Chapter Eleven
Funny Stories Make Great Material

People love to laugh and most of us do not laugh enough on a daily basis. Humor and laughter is also very good for a person, and giving an audience something "healthy" is a bonus in any presentation. In fact, recent studies indicate humor and laughter can help reduce stress, thereby, creating better blood flow to the heart, and helping to lower cholesterol. Imagine, a great presentation, and a stronger heart just for laughing – a perfect combination. The Association of Applied and Therapeutic Humor (AATH) is dedicated to understanding how therapeutic humor works and has a lot of great information for your presentations on humor and healing.

So, let's help people laugh. Another random place to look for topics is to think of funny stories that you have heard. Always make sure you cite the source when using someone else's story, but better yet, use their story to think of something similar that happened to you. **We all know that YOUR story, spoken with sincerity, is better than a story that belongs to someone else.**

There are so many funny stories that have happened in my life. If I were to give presentations based solely on the funny things that have happened in my life, I know I could talk for a very long time.

At the beginning of the book I mentioned the broken pipes in the garage and how the water flowing from the ceiling onto the irreplaceable high school yearbooks below led to presentations on protecting your valuables, but that wasn't the only speech to come out of that event. After the initial screaming from my oldest daughter, Tiffany, as she stepped out into the garage and saw the water running (and if you are a parent, you know "that" type of scream), and I realized everything was okay, we started to clean up the mess. As we were standing there going through the soggy valuables, my daughter, a fellow Toastmaster, suddenly looked at me, with great conviction, and stated, "This is MY speech, Mom." It was a very funny story.

There are a lot of funny family stories that are carried from generation to generation. Some are actually re-told with all the real facts, but most seem to be embellished over time to make them better. Another funny story from my childhood has to do with my mother deciding to buy patio furniture and temporarily forgetting she had a relatively small car. Her attempt, and success of getting this entire set of wrought iron (NOT bendable) furniture in the car, with me and my cousin, Angie (you will learn more about her in the next story), set the course for another great story. At the time, I was probably about ten years old and rather tiny, so when you picture a car full of furniture, two adults and a child, you can picture me UNDER one of the chairs, on the FLOOR of the car, curled up in a ball for the six mile ride home. Fortunately for the story, this was before the requirement for seat belts.

When I mentioned this story to my daughters, I was quickly reminded that I did something very similar to them when I purchased a full size mattress and box springs and put it in my van. There were two adults and the two of them. The girls had to lay on top of the mattress with just inches from the top of the van… for the 45 minute ride home. Hmm, I guess there is something to be said in stories about lessons we learned from our parents. Well, it is all great fun, laughter, and speech material.

To be funny, with some stories "you just had to be there" to fully understand the humor, but there are many stories that you can tell an audience and people can relate to the craziness of the moment. And, LAUGHTER IS CONTAGIOUS!

Another classic from my family involves a summer visit I had with my cousin, Angie, and my Grandmother, where I spent a lot of summer days and nights. Some of you may recall places from your childhood that were scary and you are not sure why. My Grandmother's house was always very scary to me, and I am sure that if I could see it now it would have little affect, but it was torn down after my Grandmother moved out many years ago.

One factor that I am sure made it scarier was the fact that my Grandfather, in his retirement days, worked in a big public library. When they were cleaning out some displays, they decided to get rid of a big tarantula that was preserved in formaldehyde in a large glass jar, and he thought it would be a great educational tool for the kids. Why, you are asking?? Trust me, I asked that question many times too. All I know is that most of us kids were very afraid of it.

I could start the story with... It was a dark night in a part of the city that was no stranger to crime...

The bedrooms were in a very small upstairs, just a few feet from the beloved pickled tarantula. There was a tremendous crash in the middle of the night that startled all of us from a deep sleep. It sounded like someone crashing through the kitchen windows. The first image I saw was a flashlight shining around the doorway to the bedroom. It was Angie. If I had been a cat, you would have found me hanging by my claws from the ceiling. She asked if I was okay and even at that young age I came back with a witty retort of, "I was until I saw the light. You just about scared me to death." (I say it was witty, but in all honesty I was even surprised I could speak.)

There was a very narrow staircase to the ground floor and the image of Angie leading with her small bully club in one hand and the flashlight in the other, with Grandma pushing her down the steps and me just hanging on for dear life is so vivid in my mind that it seems like it was yesterday instead of the thirty plus years ago.

We could see a glow from the kitchen as we rounded the corner. When Angie gasped, "Oh, my God", I was sure the mangled man I had envisioned in my head was lying on the floor and the sight was gruesome.

There had been a very large metal cabinet nailed to the wall above the sink. The noise was the cabinet as it came crashing down to the floor. When the cabinet fell, the noise sounded just like someone crashing through a downstairs window. The glow was from the gas stove burner that the cabinet hit as it fell. The gasp was because all of my Grandmother's dishes were smashed in what seemed like a million pieces on the floor.

The noise was so loud that the neighbors called the police and just as we were calming a bit, the police knocked on the door and the anxious feeling started all over again. The exchange between my Grandmother telling Angie she couldn't open the door in her pajamas, and Angie's always quick-witted response of, "Would you rather I take them off first?" was a perfect addition to the night.

It was a very interesting night with lost heirlooms (well, that is if you consider old jelly jars that were used for drinking glasses, heirlooms - come on, I know some of you reading this know exactly what I am talking about), wild imaginations, lots and lots of glass, a bunch of laughter, and **great speech material**!

This may be in the category of "had to be there" stories, but many years after the event, whenever I saw my Grandmother she always asked, "Do you remember the night the cabinet fell?" Then we would laugh and laugh. This went on well into her nineties and is one of the last stories she recalled the last time I saw her before her death.

Out of the Mouths of Babes

Another fun field of presentation research comes from the toddler arena.

Quick, how many of you reading this book are parents? How many of you know children? How many of you were children? (Did I catch you on that last question?) For any of you parents reading this book, you already know that children can be the basis for some of the best stories in the world with their innocence and amazement of life. If you are not a parent you can use your own childhood, or those of your family or friends to gather great material under this category.

For over 20 years, on American television, Art Linkletter brought some of the funniest scenes to life while talking with children. A child's perspective on topics ranging from parents to dancing to foods to death – it didn't seem as though any topic was left out of the dialogue. What Linkletter found, to the pleasure of his audience, was that "Kids Say the Darndest Things" (the title of a later version of the show). You can find a lot of the exchanges between Linkletter and his young guests recorded in books and film, but you don't need his show to help you realize that some of the best material indeed comes out of the mouths of babes.

What about the children around you? What lessons have they taught you? What have you observed about how children respond to humor vs. the adults around them? Have you ever just sat and watched children play and admired the wonderful imagination enjoyed by children? Has it inspired you to watch a child sleep? Children have so much to teach adults, and this can be the basis for some great presentations on humor, inspiration and love.

Out of the Mouths of Babes: The next time you have an opportunity to observe children, take the time to really think about a message that can be gleaned from their innocence and amazement of the world around them. Identify some lessons learned and what the lessons can teach your audience.

1. _____

      Point 1: _____

      Point 2: _____

      Point 3: _____

2. _____

      Point 1: _____

      Point 2: _____

      Point 3: _____

3. _____

      Point 1: _____

      Point 2: _____

      Point 3: _____

4. _____

      Point 1: _____

      Point 2: _____

      Point 3: _____

Made up stories can be another great source of fun for presentations. Sweet Maggie that I mention in the previous chapter was a flat coated retriever, but before we knew her breed we decided to make one up for her. She looked like a black Labrador Retriever with a fluffy tail but had the black markings of a Chow tongue. Since we thought she was a Chow-Lab mix, we started to tell people she was a Chabix. One day we went into a major pet store chain with Maggie. A woman came up to us and asked what breed of dog she was. Without missing a beat, I told her she was a Chabix, a rare breed from the British Isles. The woman looked her over from head to tail and emphatically stated that Maggie was a "fine specimen of her breed, indeed". My daughter had to walk away she was laughing so hard! We have a wonderful family story to share, but it has also become part of a humorous presentation on the dangers of trying to "con" someone when you don't really know the answers.

Another TRUE story that I always like to use when talking about humor is about my friend, Carol. Carol was not known to be a very good cook and she got tired of the constant teasing from her family. One Thanksgiving she decided she was going to impress the family. After they all went to a restaurant for the main dinner, Carol would have everyone over to her place for dessert. Carol was certain she could at least bake a cake, after all, how hard is it to follow the instructions on a cake mix?

She did just what it said on the box. She mixed all of the ingredients and *greased the bottom of the pan*. She wasn't sure why the box said to grease the bottom of the pan, but she thought maybe the pan would slide in and out of the oven easier that way. Think about it. This is a true story!

Funny stories are everywhere. For some they aren't easy to spot, for others the stories are everywhere, and it seems like some family members just attract funny stories. Whichever way it is with your family and friends, cherish the moments, then talk about them. Laughter IS contagious!

Funny Stories: What about you, what are some funny stories that have happened to you and how can you use this information for the basis of a great presentation? On the blanks below, record some funny stories and name three things could you use as part of your story.

1. _____

      Point 1: _____

      Point 2: _____

      Point 3: _____

2. _____

      Point 1: _____

      Point 2: _____

      Point 3: _____

3. _____

      Point 1: _____

      Point 2: _____

      Point 3: _____

4. _____

      Point 1: _____

      Point 2: _____

      Point 3: _____

Added Challenge: This is a GREAT activity for your next family function. Take your list, or make a new, longer one to your next family event and see how many stories you can generate under this category. You may be surprised by how many stories are related, and by some of the "details" of the stories.

Family Generated Stories:

Who told it? _____ When? _____

1. _____

       Point 1: _____

       Point 2: _____

       Point 3: _____

Who told it? _____ When? _____

2. _____

       Point 1: _____

       Point 2: _____

       Point 3: _____

Who told it? _____ When? _____

3. _____

       Point 1: _____

       Point 2: _____

       Point 3: _____

Notes and Key Points From This Chapter:

Chapter Twelve
Just to Quote a Few

I like to use quotes to either inspire entire presentations or to add related material to a presentation. In the later section on Image Mapping, Chapter Eighteen, there are several examples of adding quotes as supporting material for your presentation.

You can find quotes relating to almost any topic and by all types of people, from the famous to the not as famous. Again, that term "famous" is very subjective so don't forget to use quotes or favorite sayings from your family members.

You can use one or two quotes to set the points of your presentation, or a series of quotes as we do in the Image Mapping on Leadership.

For example, we could give a presentation relating to embracing the moment and use the following quotes…

American writer, Ernestine Ulmer, may have been the first one to say, "Life is uncertain, eat dessert first", but my mother, Ruth Miller, has used these words as a motto for her life. She is firm believer that you never know what might happen during dinner, so you should always eat your dessert first.

*Steve Wilson, of the World Laughter Tour, agrees with this sentiment and often coins the phrase, "Don't postpone joy". In his book, **Good Hearted Living**, Steve, uses this phrase as a personal mantra to remind himself and others that each day is filled with brief moments that can be gone before we know it, so embrace the joy around you and make sure you do not postpone the happiness you find with family, friends, and experiences.*

We could use these two quotes to introduce the topic of embracing the day, then continue to talk about stories or experiences of people who take advantage of every moment in time, and the realization that we only walk this way once in life, and we do not get a second chance for that "once in a lifetime" opportunity.

Quotes allow us to introduce ideas and thoughts of other people without losing ourselves in the stories of someone else. Sometimes it is difficult to know the true origin of a quote, but whenever possible, make sure you cite the source. In this section, let's look at some quotes and how some of these quotes could be used as the basis for a presentation.

In this chapter we are going to look at twenty quotes from a variety of people and topics. We will look at possible presentation points for five of the quotes, then as the activity for the chapter, select at least five more from the list and develop your own presentations.

Added challenge: As you are reading the quote, and before reading my suggestions, think of what you would talk about based on the stated quote.

1. American President Franklin D. Roosevelt once said, **"Be sincere; be brief; be seated."** (A personal favorite for some speakers I know.)
> Possible topics: How to Give a Good Speech; What is Toastmasters International; and The Powerful Words of Franklin Roosevelt

Sometimes you do not know the author, as in a few quotes by that famous author, Anonymous, who said.....

2. **"Remember, people will judge you by your actions, not your intentions. You may have a heart of gold -- but so does a hard-boiled egg."**

Possible topics: Service Organizations vs. Social Organizations; The History of Rotary International; and You Do Not Have to be A Millionaire to be a Philanthropist

3. *"Count your age with friends but not with years."*
Possible topics: My Best Friends are Dogs; How to be Your Own Best Friend; and Stories from Childhood Friends

4. *"A closed mind is a good thing to lose."*
Possible topics: Communication is the Key to World Peace; The Devastation of Alzheimer's on a Family; and How to be Persuasive

Sometimes there are words of wisdom passed down from generation to generation as in an old Irish Proverb:

5. *"You've got to do your own growing, no matter how tall your grandfather was."*
Possible topics: How Andrew Carnegie's Library Contributions Changed the World; Lessons I Learned from My Grandfather; and Coal Mining in Kentucky (my Grandfather was a coal miner)

Many great presentations have started with quotes from the Bible or other valuable books, such as:

6. *"To every thing there is a season."* - Ecclesiastes 3. 1-8

7. *"Do not let any unwholesome talk come out of your mouths, but only what is helpful for building others up according to their needs, that it may benefit those who listen."* – Ephesians 4:29

You know I had to have a quote from Dolly Parton, a very outspoken woman who inspires all kinds of presentations.
8. *"Just because I am soft and sexy, don't ever make the mistake of thinking I am stupid."*

There are quotes from all types of people, some we know, and some we may not.

9. *"Some men are born great, some achieve greatness, and some have greatness thrust upon them."*
William Shakespeare

10. American writer, Mark Twain once said, *"It usually takes more than three weeks to write a good impromptu speech."* (I wonder what he would have thought of our Speech Cookie OREO Method?)

11. *"In all the universe, in all time, you are the only you. Never have molecules come together exactly like you; never again will your footsteps be repeated upon this earth. Your strength is the strength someone can count on, your life is the life that can make a difference."*
Author Unknown

12. *"If you hear a voice within you say 'you cannot paint', then by all means paint, and that voice will be silenced."*
Vincent Van Gogh

13. *"Fools live to regret their words; wise men to regret their silence."*
Will Henry

14. *"You miss 100 percent of the shots you never take."*
Wayne Gretzky

15. *"Live your life so that you would not be ashamed to sell the family parrot to the town gossip."*
Will Rogers (I love this one!)

16. *"Nothing in the future will correct those moments you have missed in the past."*
Author Unknown

17. *"Think what a better world it would be if we all, the whole world, had cookies and milk about three o'clock every afternoon and then lay down on our blankets for a nap."*
Barbara Jordan

18. *"There is no passion to be found playing small - in settling for a life that is less than the one you are capable of living."*
Nelson Mandela

19. *"You will be the same person in five years as you are today except for the people you meet and the books you read."*
Charlie "Tremendous" Jones

20. *"When you have a dream, you've got to grab it and never let go."* or *"I don't have false teeth. Do you think I'd buy teeth like these?"*
Carol Burnett

Bonus: *"You cannot always control what happens to you, but what you can control is how you respond to it."*
Tammy A. Miller

To Quote a Few: We have looked at possible presentation topics for five of the quotes, please select at least five more from the list and develop your own presentations.

1. Quote: _____

_____

    Point 1: _____

    Point 2: _____

    Point 3: _____

2. Quote: _____

_____

      Point 1: _____

      Point 2: _____

      Point 3: _____

3. Quote: _____

_____

      Point 1: _____

      Point 2: _____

      Point 3: _____

4. Quote: _____

_____

      Point 1: _____

      Point 2: _____

      Point 3: _____

5. Quote: _____

_____

      Point 1: _____

      Point 2: _____

      Point 3: _____

Notes and Key Points From This Chapter:

_____

_____

_____

_____

_____

_____

_____

_____

_____

_____

_____

_____

_____

_____

_____

_____

Chapter Thirteen
Fortune Cookie

Another place to look for inspiration, but in a tastier form is using fortune cookies as the basis for presentations. In this chapter we are going to look at twenty actual fortune cookie fortunes (thanks to my favorite Chinese restaurant in State College, PA, The Golden Wok). We will look at possible presentation points for five of the fortunes, then as the activity for the chapter, select at least five more from the list and develop your own presentations.

Added challenge: As you are reading the fortune, and before reading my suggestions, think of what you would talk about based on the fortune.

1. **You will always get what you want through your charm and personality.**
> Possible topics: Personality Types; How to Tell When Someone is Lying; and Lessons I Learned in Charm School

2. **A financial investment will yield returns beyond your hopes.**
> Possible topics: Financial Investing for Beginners; Do Men and Women Have Different Financial Needs; and How to Buy Property as an Investment

3. **To live your life in fear of losing it is to lose the point of life.**
> Possible topics: Is Public Speaking Really the Number One Fear; How to Make Each Day Count; and Jump Out of the Plane, You Only Live Once

4. **There is nothing lost or wasted in this life.**
> Possible topics: Why We Should Recycle; Lessons Learned Each Day; and Education Can Never Be Taken Away

5. Today is the tomorrow we worried about yesterday.
Possible topics: The Value of Worry; What is the Worse Thing That Can Happen Today?; and The History of the Calendar

6. Our purpose in life is not to get ahead of other people – but to get ahead of ourselves.

7. Success comes with self-acceptance.

8. We create our fate everyday we live.

9. Wise sayings often fall on barren ground, but a kind word is never thrown away.

10. This is an extremely favorable day, just perfect for romance.

11. Go with the flow will make your transition ever so much easier.

12. Take advantage of the dynamic energy to better your relationship.

13. You have a natural grace and great consideration for others.

14. All your hard work will soon pay off.

15. The first step to better times is to imagine them.

16. Better a diamond with a flaw than a pebble without one.

17. Accept something that you cannot change and you will feel better.

18. Self knowledge is a life long process.

19. **Your life will get more and more exciting.**

20. **In order to take one must first give.**

If you get a chance the next time you are in State College, PA, stop by and see Julie and her family at the Golden Wok, and tell her Tammy sent you. I am sure you will get a fortune cookie or two and it may just be the great beginning for your next incredible presentation.

Fortune Cookie Topics: We have looked at possible presentation topics for five of the fortunes, please select at least five more from the list and develop your own presentations.

1. Fortune: _____

_____

      Point 1: _____

      Point 2: _____

      Point 3: _____

2. Fortune: _____

_____

      Point 1: _____

      Point 2: _____

      Point 3: _____

3. Fortune: _____

_____

      Point 1: _____

      Point 2: _____

      Point 3: _____

4. Fortune: _____

_____

      Point 1: _____

      Point 2: _____

      Point 3: _____

5. Fortune: _____

_____

      Point 1: _____

      Point 2: _____

      Point 3: _____

Notes and Key Points From This Chapter:

Chapter Fourteen
Look Around the Room

If you were to just sit in your home, office, or apartment, you would most likely be able to view over one hundred items, just by glancing around the room. For example, as I look around my office, I see a wide range of office supplies. These supplies include a stapler, tape, paper clips, scissors, and paper, to name a few. Of course, by now, you know that I am not just seeing "items", but possible topics for future presentations. I hope that by this point in the book, you are seeing these items in this light, too. Just seeing them and thinking about what we can talk about is great, but if we write down a few, we are that much closer to our full presentation. I will start with a few examples, and then offer plenty of space for you to consider a few items.

From the Office:

Stapler
> History (always a great place to start); Surgical Uses; and Craft Projects Using a Stapler

Scissors
> Early Manufacturing; Why We Should Have a Pair of Kitchen Shears; and the movie, Edward Scissorhands

Tape
> Types of Tape; Crazy Uses of Duct Tape; and Manufacturing of Tape

Pen/Pencil
> Collecting; Value; and Designs

Computer
> Size: From a Large Room to Your Hand; Basic Computer Skills; and How to Assemble Your Own Computer

From the Kitchen:

Can Opener
> Manual vs. Electric – Which Do Your Prefer?; What's Your Favorite Kitchen Gadget; and The History of the Tin Can

Microwave
> From Large Box to Tiny Power; Is Microwaved Food Healthy; and Using Your Microwave to Sterilize

Toaster
> Elements of a Tiny Oven; My Best Friends are Crumbs; and New Advances on Muffin Making

Cabinets
> Storage for Everyday Items; New Cabinets vs. Resurfacing; and A Place for Everything

Silverware
> Eating Utensils Throughout History; Is There Really Silver in Silverware; and Favorite Finger Foods

I remember a very informative and persuasive presentation about the differences between a top loading and a front loading washing machine. When I am in the market for another washer, I will seriously consider the front loader, just because of this presentation.

We just listed another 30 topics (or 31 if you would like to research the washing machine) for your next presentation. If you aren't sure what to talk about when you get the main topic idea, a quick Mind Map (Chapter Nineteen), or Topic Tier (Chapter Twenty), will give you even more ideas to explore.

Added Challenge: Do this activity with at least three rooms for even more ideas.

Look Around the Room: Take a look around the room you are sitting in and identify at least four items that you could use as a foundation for a presentation, and at least three things you could talk about with each item.

1. _____

    Point 1: _____

    Point 2: _____

    Point 3: _____

2. _____

    Point 1: _____

    Point 2: _____

    Point 3: _____

3. _____

    Point 1: _____

    Point 2: _____

    Point 3: _____

4. _____

    Point 1: _____

    Point 2: _____

    Point 3: _____

Notes and Key Points From This Chapter:

_____

_____

_____

_____

_____

_____

_____

_____

_____

_____

_____

_____

_____

_____

_____

_____

_____

Chapter Fifteen
Random Thoughts to Real Life Talks

So far we have used a variety of ways to develop topics for presentations, including life successes, challenges we have met, lessons learned from life, people we have met, songs for inspiration, and quotes, to select a few. There are several other ways to develop topics that will be included in this chapter, in no particular order, but each idea offers many more topics from which to choose.

Magazine articles: There are a lot of great magazines available that are filled with good information for your next presentation. A couple of my personal favorites are *Reader's Digest and Guideposts*. I like these two in particular because they are portable and are filled with short stories that inspire me and other presentations. My favorite for speech material comes from the magazine, *Mental Floss*. This bi-monthly magazine is filled with fun, astounding, surprising, endearing, you name it…information that is a perfect place to gain and gather all kinds of great speech material.

Books: Books of all kinds are another favorite place to look for material. I have given several presentations based on the wonderful library of that ultimate philosopher, Dr. Seuss.

As a child I loved fairy tales. As I have grown older, I still love fairy tales, but have now used the messages contained in these fairy tales as the basis of many empowering presentations. One of my favorite presentations is titled, *Mirror, Mirror, On the Wall*. This presentation is about who we *really* see when we look in the mirror and how we can change who we see, if we choose to do so.

Maybe check out the best seller list and see what develops, or get a copy of *Chase's Calendar of Events* for a lot of fun.

It's a sign

This is one of my favorite activities as I am traveling. I love to read signs, especially on church billboards or marquees that have a different saying each week. Even when I am traveling the same road to the office, each Monday or Tuesday morning the sign is changed and I play a "What kind of speech would this sign make?" game. I know, I know, some of you are thinking that I have no life, but this is a great creativity activity. Some of my favorites are:

We don't need more to be thankful for, we need to be more thankful

We Are Not Dairy Queen...But We Have Great Sundays

Souler energy used here

A closed mouth gathers no foot

Church parking only. Violators will be baptized

Forgive your enemies, it will mess with their mind

Get rich quick. Count your blessings.

Failure is success if we learn from it

Fill your years with life, not your life with years

Integrity is who you are when the light is out

Don't let the littleness in others bring out the littleness in you

Pessimists need a kick in the can'ts

Sign broken - come inside for messages

Live life as an exclamation, not an explanation

Triumph is just UMPH added to TRY.

Smile often. If your face hurts, then you are out of shape

Look not behind or ahead, but within

Making excuses doesn't change the truth

Laugh a lot, especially at yourself

It's a Sign Topics: Similar to the quote and fortune cookies, use at least three of these signs and see what type of presentation you could develop.

1. Sign: _____

     Point 1: _____

     Point 2: _____

     Point 3: _____

2. Sign: _____

     Point 1: _____

     Point 2: _____

     Point 3: _____

3. Sign: _____

     Point 1: _____

     Point 2: _____

     Point 3: _____

Simply random: This is just a random list of some thought generators as you continue to assemble your topic notebook.

Family Adventures
Passions
Talents
Values
Crazy Holidays
Lessons from your favorite television show
Type any word in an internet search engine
Truth is stranger than fiction
The most beautiful place you have visited
Storytelling the characters of the Bible
Your favorite acronyms
Do a whole speech using just book titles
Creating a gratitude list
Your favorite movies as inspiration

Complete the sentences to a complete presentation

If I won the lottery today…
I share my birthday with…
My top three favorite movies are…
This is what brings me joy…
My perfect day is…
The funniest thing that has ever happened to me…

Notes and Key Points From This Chapter:

_____

_____

_____

_____

_____

_____

_____

_____

_____

_____

_____

_____

_____

Chapter Sixteen
The Basic Structure

Now that we have looked at several ways to develop topics, let's spend more time discussing the various structures you can use. In Chapter Three we discussed the thought process of **Thinking in Threes**. This set us up for a way to think about any topic or item, and by thinking of at least three things we could talk about, we could develop a presentation using the simple structure of:

Introduction
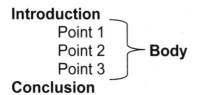
    Point 1
    Point 2   **Body**
    Point 3
Conclusion

Some people like to say...
    1. Tell them what you are going to tell them
    2. Tell them
    3. Tell them what you told them

This is a pretty simple statement for looking at:
    1. Tell them what you are going to tell them
        (INTRODUCTION)
    2. Tell them
        (BODY)
    3. Tell them what you told them
        (CONCLUSION)
but, it doesn't offer a lot of solid foundational material to help you understand these three key components of an effective presentation very well, and since I have a few pages devoted to this chapter, let's see if we can fill in between the lines a bit.

BONUS: Keep in mind that this structure and the information in this chapter is not just for a speech but can also be an excellent structure when giving a project brief, speaking in a meeting, or even writing. Once you understand the key concepts, it will be helpful to you in many areas of life that you may not even realize at this moment.

<u>Introduction</u>

A solid speech introduction will often determine whether or not your audience continues to listen to the rest of your presentation. You want to make the audience **want** to listen to your presentation. It is the first impression, *verbally*, that the audience has of you and it must grab and maintain their attention. (There is a great deal of research that indicates that an audience is already deciding, on some level, to listen to your presentation or not, within the first 10 seconds that they SEE you – before you even open your mouth. This can be based on what was said in the introduction that someone read about you, your appearance, the situation or other factors. The idea about first impressions would make a great topic for a presentation.)

Just to be clear, the concept of the *introduction* that we are discussing here is the *speech introduction*. If you are in a position where someone is verbally introducing you to the audience, that type of introduction is different. This is a key part of your presentation, though, so make sure it is strong and concise. I always recommend to speakers that the introduction is clearly typed, in large, readable font, and you give a copy to the presenter in advance so they have an opportunity to review it for clarification, and have an extra copy with you at the time of your presentation, just in case it is needed. Also, make sure you *listen* to the introduction. There have been many cases where a speaker is depending on information in the introduction to help set-up their presentation, and if the introducer does not say it to the audience, then the speaker must adapt the related material. There are a lot of good resources available to help you write a solid introduction for this purpose. If you have any questions on this, please contact me.

Your presentation introduction should be brief, making up only 10 – 15% of the entire presentation.

There are multiple elements that go into an effective introduction including:

Gain attention of your audience
Establish your credibility
Preview the presentation

Gain Attention

There are several ways to gain attention, including:

Storytelling: A story may be a very effective way to open your presentation. If you choose to start with a story, it needs to, *not just related* to the topic, but **add value** to the points, and be brief. If you have other points in your presentation and you open with a long story, your audience will get lost in the story and may not recognize the point you are trying to make, or understand your *specific message*. A story about your day in the garden has no value in a presentation about the best ink blends for printing a book, unless the inks are made from something in the garden.

The story should be short and to the point. If you have to use a lot of set-up for an entire cast of characters, the story is too long for the introduction, and you may have lost the audience.

If you are telling a story as the entire presentation, then great detail may be required for your audience to be able to "see" the characters, but in the introduction too much detail may detract from the rest of the message. An example of this would be if you are giving a presentation about the importance of having a living will (if you are not familiar with this term, look it up and present the information). If you are using a story about a person who had a life threatening illness and did not have a living will, it would be more effective to place the audience in a "typical day" like a Sunday afternoon. *"It was a Sunday afternoon, with the sun shining and the birds singing. John and Joan were enjoying a leisurely breakfast at the kitchen table when suddenly, John collapsed onto the kitchen floor"*, is more effective than, "It was Sunday, July 10, 1978....". When you use a date, your audience is immediately taken back to the date and trying to recall where they may have been at the time and not listening to what you are saying...they are *wandering*, and the detail may not be necessary to the message. Stories can be a great way to gain the attention of your audience, regardless of the type of presentation you are giving, and can be very effective if you keep all of these key elements in mind for opening with a story.

Questions: Asking a question or a couple of questions to engage the audience can be an effective opener. Like a story, the questions should be brief, to the point and directly related to the information you are about to present. A word of caution when asking a question of your audience, especially when you are trying to persuade on what may be a controversial issue; if you are expecting to persuade your audience, and you want to open with a question, it is best to know how the audience will respond to the question before it is asked. For example, if you think you are going to have a difficult time persuading the audience and you open with a question to gauge their position on the topic and they all agree with you, two things have happened, you did not do a thorough job of analyzing your audience, and you may be wasting everyone's time with the presentation.

Make a powerful statement: This can be especially effective if you are giving a persuasive presentation and you want to really add impact for the audience. For example, if you were giving a presentation on underage drinking, you might start with, "Mom, it's Sarah, I have been arrested and I am in jail." This statement is more powerful than opening with, "Underage drinking is not a good thing."

114

Establish Your Credibility

Credibility is the level of perceived trustworthiness and expertise that a speaker brings to an audience. If you were going to hear a presentation about, *The Key Elements of Good Comedy*, would you more likely want to hear Carol Burnett (or insert your favorite comedian here ☺) or Bill Gates talk about the subject? You may go to hear Bill Gates, just because you are intrigued by what this seemingly serious computer guy knows about comedy, but more likely you would want to hear from a woman who has devoted much of her life to making people laugh as a comedian. If you do not recognize either of these names, the biographies of both of them are readily available and would make a great informative presentation. The two of them would make a great presentation with the contrast structure (Chapter Seventeen), too.

In this situation, you may already know the names of the people I mentioned, and by association sensed the level of credibility that the speaker would bring to the topic, but in more everyday terms, your audience may not know who you are or what makes you the authority on the given topic. If this is the case, then your introduction is a great place to tell them.

This is not a time to tout all of your lofty accolades, but rather a quick one or two sentence statement as to why you are the expert on this topic on this day. It can be as simple as, *"For the past ten years I have been involved with search and rescue teams in devastated areas. I have flown over 20 goodwill missions to areas struck by natural disasters, and today I am here to talk to you about how you can get involved in helping others affected by natural disasters."* This quick couple of statements lets the audience know that this person may be an expert in the field of helping others through natural disasters. (By the language, would you expect this to be an informative presentation or persuasive? The phrase, "how you can get involved" indicates the speaker is offering a persuasive presentation and will provide us with the necessary tools for the *call to action*.) Your credibility may be in the fact that you have researched a topic, lived through a situation, worked in the topic field, studied in school, went through a challenge, etc., whatever it takes to let your audience know that you are capable of speaking in an educated manner about the topic.

Preview the Presentation

Where are you taking your audience? The preview that you offer your audience in the introduction serves a dual purpose. It tells your audience where you are going to take them with the presentation, and it also helps you know the path you are taking. Like the credibility statement, this is also very brief, just introducing the points, not talking in detail about the points, as that will be done in the body of the presentation. For example, if you are using the three point system, and your topic is underage drinking you could say, *"In this presentation, we will look at the statistics of underage drinking; what is already being done to help eliminate the problem; and how you can get involved today to make a difference."* (Can you identify what type of presentation it is – informative vs. persuasive? The statement, "how you can get involved today to make a difference" tells us it is persuasive in nature and the speaker is asking for a call to action to make a difference.)

Many people find it most helpful to write the introduction after completing the body and conclusion. This makes perfect sense in the way that you will have a clearer understanding of what you are going to say, and part of that introduction is telling the audience where you are going to take them.

Another helpful tip for the introduction is to consider writing it out completely. This is especially helpful for people who are nervous or new to speaking opportunities. By writing out your introduction, and reading or memorizing it, you may gain more confidence as you proceed into the body of the presentation. I am not a strong advocate for memorizing your presentations, but that will be a topic for the next book ☺.

Pay great attention to the introduction as you pull your audience in with you and invite them to join you on the journey.

Body

The largest part of your presentation is the body and requires the most work to make sure that your points are clear, concise and thoroughly relate your specific message to the audience.

In this chapter we are looking at a simple, straightforward three point structure for the body of the presentation, but the next chapter addresses several other structures you can consider for building the body of the presentation. These structures include:

Straight Information
Comparison
Contrast
Cause/Effect
Problem/Solution
Timeline or Sequence of Events
Time in Threes
Ordered Pieces
Whole in Steps

Each structure is defined in much greater detail in the next chapter, so you can get a better idea of the several structure options available for the message you are presenting.

Regardless of which structure you choose, there are foundational elements that you need in the body of your presentation.

Relate to the Specific Message: Each point needs to relate to the specific message you desire to convey in the message. This may seem elementary but, without a direct connection to the specific message, a point can relate to the topic but not have the *added value* needed to be appropriate. For example, if you are presenting a persuasive presentation to your local government and you want them to give you funding to present Emergency Medical Technician (EMT) classes in the community, your specific message may be:

I want my audience to provide appropriate funding so that I can conduct Emergency Medical Technician (EMT) courses to community members.

If you are using the three point structure, you may choose as your points for this persuasive presentation:

1. Statistics relating to current emergency calls
2. The lack of qualified ambulance drivers and technicians
3. The amount of funding needed and how it would be used

Another point that could be used when talking about EMT training would be visiting impoverished countries to provide medical services. While this is a valid point that people who are trained in EMT services may consider, it is not a related point to your specific message in *this* presentation, and would not be a valid point in this persuasive message.

Relate to the Audience: The way you put the body together is very much tied to the audience hearing the message. For example, if we use Jamey & Molly's presentation from Chapter Six, the way they structure the body of the presentation can be adapted to relate to the audience.

If they are focusing on the high level of effective communication required in the situation and delivering the message to a Toastmasters audience, then they will choose their points so that each point will emphasize some element relating to the need for communication.

If they are focusing on the divine intervention they felt at several points along the way and delivering the message to a faith based audience, then each point will relate to the intervention of a higher power.

If they are focusing on the role that a positive attitude played in Molly's recovery from the surgeries and ultimate use of prosthetics, then each point will have elements of how a positive attitude made a difference.

The points that they are building and making throughout the presentation will be tailored to the specific audience. A review from Chapter Four of the elements of audience analysis:

1. What is my audience expecting?
2. What do they already know about the topic?
3. How is the audience going to use your information?
4. What do you have in common with your audience?
5. Are demographics an issue (age, race, religion, location of audience, background, etc.)
6. If this is a persuasive presentation, how do they already feel about the topic?
7. If you are persuading the audience, are there key points that you know they are against and what are you using to alleviate these concerns?

Mark Brown, 1995 World Champion of Public Speaking, states that, "Great speeches are not written, they are assembled into a package that people cannot resist." This statement is about making sure you understand your specific message; your audience understands what you are trying to convey, and the points within the body are related to the message and audience.

Building Your Points: In the same manner that we have used several methods to develop topics, you have several methods available to build your points. Once you developed the main points, then each point can be further developed by using a straight brainstorming method or the Mind Mapping technique, as we discuss in Chapter Nineteen or the Topic Tiers method as described in Chapter Twenty. All of these methods will help you put more "meat on the bones" of your presentation (another great speech topic – the history of crazy phrases).

Supporting Materials: There are several types of supporting materials you can use in the body of your presentation.

Quotes: In Chapter Twelve on developing presentations by using quotes as the starting point, we briefly discussed using quotes in your presentation. A quote is an excellent way to reinforce your point by using the words of someone else, and is especially effective if the person you are quoting is considered an expert in the topic field. For example, if you were doing a presentation on leadership, a quote by Stephen Covey, author of the bestseller, **The Seven Habits of Highly Effective People**, **The 8th Habit**, and other books, would offer a stronger support to your presentation than Joe, your well known and well respected local plumber.

This is one of my favorite Covey quotes from **The 8th Habit**:

"Leadership is communicating to people their worth and potential so clearly that they come to see it in themselves."

However, if you are giving a presentation about household repairs and you quote related information from Joe, then it would be more effective than Steven Covey, because you are quoting an expert in the field. Steven Covey may very well know a lot about plumbing, but he is not known as an expert in the field.

Statistics: Anyone who knows me well knows that I am not a numbers person, unless I am calculating the "percentage off" during a sale at the local store – then, I am an expert. (In fact, this is how my daughters learned percentages – while we were shopping, if they could figure it out – I would buy it. This only worked until they got good at it though, then I had to stop and save the bank.) However, statistics can play a vital role in your supporting material, if they are handled properly.

Statistics need to be clear and concise and *directly related* to your message. If you are giving a presentation about recycling in your community, a statistic about how much waste goes into your local community landfill will reinforce your point. A statistic about the landfill in another town may be fine, but if it is not directly related to your message, do not use it.

Statistics should also be used sparingly and always cite the source. Unless you are an accountant, or just simply love numbers, most people do not want to sit through any presentation that is just a series of numbers after numbers. For a three point presentation, a good rule may be a maximum of 2-3 statistics per point.

Explain the numbers and only use what is relevant to your points. A clear, legible chart showing just the numbers you are referring to can be very helpful to the audience. A good gauge of using a statistic is to make sure your audience would clearly understand the statistic, and how it was related if there weren't any visual aids used to show the information. Can you verbally express the numbers and have them make sense to your audience?

Examples: There are many types of examples that you can use as supporting material. Examples could be stories, yours or someone else's; they could be testimony from experts in the field you are presenting; or they could be reinforcing the point or making it clearer for the audience.

For whatever purpose you are using the example, make sure it is clear why you are using this example and, as with the others, examples need to be clear and concise.

Questions: Asking questions can be an important part of your body, as well as the introduction. While this is more of a delivery technique to keep your audience engaged, you should think of questions you can ask your audience in the body of the presentation while you are developing your points. Asking your audience questions that tie them to the material will help them with self reflection and relating their experiences to what you are talking about. A word of caution with questions, always give your audience time to think about the answer in their own minds. It does not have to be a very long time, but if you ask the question and immediately continue talking you are stepping on their thoughts. We have all left presentations wanting to hear more of the story, or material because it was so good, and there have been a few that we were relieved when the speaker was finished. What is the difference? A solid body of information presented.

Conclusion

You have provided a powerful introduction to the presentation. You have delivered a body that kept your audience engaged throughout. Now, you are wrapping up the whole package. The purpose of the conclusion is to put the bow on the package!

There are several elements of an effective conclusion:

Be Brief: The conclusion should only be about 5 – 10% of the entire presentation.

The End of the Journey: In the introduction, you invited the audience to join you on a journey. Now you are letting the audience know the journey is ending. There is a fine line between leaving your audience wanting more and keeping them satisfied with what you delivered. The conclusion plays a role in the audience satisfaction. Did you just end, or did you pull it all together for the audience?

Reinforce and Review: The conclusion offers you an opportunity to reinforce the specific message you wanted to impart to your audience. You can reinforce your message with a concluding review of your main message. Referring back to your introduction can be a powerful way to pull the information all together. For example, if you opened with a story, connect the conclusion back to a key part of your story.

No New Information: The introduction can introduce new information; the body can introduce new information; but the conclusion should only work with material you have already presented. Remember, you are reinforcing in the conclusion.

Be Creative: Leave your audience thinking about something. Regardless of whether your intent is to Inform, Persuade, Motivate, Inspire, or Entertain, the conclusion offers you an opportunity to leave your audience thinking about something. How can you leave your audience thinking about something of value because they listened to what you had to say? Can you leave them with an image, a picture in their head, a powerful quote, empowered to do something, to make a change, to make a difference? Think about this element as you are researching your topic and putting your points together.

WOW! A lot of information packed into this chapter. The structure is vital to an effective presentation and can be the difference between an okay presentation, a good presentation and a fantastic presentation. Go for the gold!

Added Considerations

Transition Statements: In addition to the straight structure indicated at the beginning of this chapter, it is also important to place transition statements as you are moving from one place to the next. To better indicate this, let's change the structure to include the transition statements so that the diagram looks like this:

Introduction
    Transition to Point 1
    Point 1
    Transition to Point 2
    Point 2   **Body**
    Transition to Point 3
    Point 3
    Transition to Conclusion
Conclusion

The purpose of the transition statement is to simply transition the information, audience and you from one part of the presentation to the other. The transition statement does not have to be complicated, and is usually one or two sentences.

If we borrow a topic from Chapter Fourteen and we are talking about staplers, and the three points are:
1. The History of the Stapler
2. Surgical Uses for the Stapler
3. Craft Projects Using a Stapler
A simple example would be, "*Now that we have looked at the history of the stapler, let's explore some of the surgical uses of the stapler.*" It is simply a signpost that is helping to keep the direction of the presentation moving forward.

The transition statements provide an internal review of what you have talked about, and the final transition indicates that you are coming to the end of your presentation. There are a lot of ways to transition to the conclusion including:

In summary…
In the final analysis…
As we end out time today…
To bring this to a close…

Your main goal with the transition statements is to keep the information flowing smoothly.

KEY CONCEPT – No Wandering: This book does not go into detail on the actual delivery of the presentation, which may be for the next book☺, but I ask that you keep one very important element in mind when you are thinking about putting your presentation together. Be very careful about using jargon or lingo (a vocabulary used by a particular group), unexplained acronyms, dates, numbers, or ANYTHING that may cause your audience to allow their minds to "wander" to figure out something that you said.

It is important to point out this key element that can help you keep your audience with you and more engaged. **Anytime your audience is trying to figure out something that you said, they are not paying attention to you.**

For example, if you say you were born in 1972, the audience is immediately trying to figure out how old you are and they have "left you" for a few moments. By contrast, if you state your age as 37 years old, the audience continues to move right along with you through the next sentence.

You often hear this in presentations (and meetings) when someone is talking and using lingo or what they think are common phrases. In many cases, not everyone in the audience understands exactly what you are talking about, and the wandering may begin.

If you have to use abbreviations, acronyms, or lingo, make sure you identify the full statement at least once and say that you will be referring to it by the abbreviation for the rest of your presentation. An example of this would be the term

COD. If you do an internet search for the meaning of the acronym COD, you will find over 70 possible meanings for the term (this would be a great speech topic), including Collect on Delivery, Cash on Delivery, Certificate of Deposit, or even Coffee of the Day, just to name a few. Always make sure you define the term or phrase first, note what term or phrase you will be using for future reference, then you can use just the acronym. This method will keep your audience on the path with you.

This idea is vitally important in the introduction when you are asking the audience to really give you their full attention, but equally important at any point in your presentation. **If the mind of your audience member is wandering, he/she is not paying attention to you.** Don't make them work for the information that you can lay out for them. Throughout the presentation, be as concise and descriptive as possible. Keep your audience with you at all times.

As to your audience wandering to think about their grocery list or "To Do" list, well, one step at a time. If you stay focused on the information in this chapter, I am sure you will keep them right with you at all times.

Exercising your mind

The exercise in this chapter is adapted from a very interactive exercise I do in person. Let's start by brainstorming some wild and crazy topics. The reason I use "crazy" topics is to demonstrate how we can put a presentation together with ANY topic and how you could easily adapt this method for topics for which you have familiarity. To give you an idea, I will borrow a few that have been suggested in classes I have taught, here is a list:
1. Flying squirrels
2. Cheese
3. Pickles
4. Body piercing
5. Ink Pens

Maybe you would like to think of a few more.

1. _____

2. _____

3. _____

Your exercise is to choose a crazy topic and decide how you would put it together. You may want to do a Mind Map, Topic Tier (Chapters Nineteen and Twenty) or a brainstorm list to decide your points.

For example, let's choose cheese. You could talk about types, health benefits, ageing process, colors, flavors, origins, calories, textures, making, pizza, foods, and uses.

Think of at least three elements from EACH part of the structure that you could use for this project. These do not have to be complete sentences. You could use a couple of words to help you "see" the information in your own mind. For example with cheese as the topic:

I want my audience to understand more about the types of cheeses, the ageing process, and why they should eat cheese as a healthy addition to their diet.

<u>Introduction</u>
1. Sniff in the air with pleasure; sniff in the air with disgust
2. Studied cheese for past 10 years
3. Preview types; ageing process; and health benefits

<u>Body</u>

Point 1: Types
1. Blue cheese – really mold?
2. Cheddar cheese - orange
3. Swiss Cheese - white

Point 2: Ageing process
1. Salt
2. Temperature
3. Moisture

Point 3: Health Benefits
1. Strong bones
2. Mom's story
3. Great teeth

Conclusion
1. Review
2. Provide a variety of cheese to taste
3. Sniff in the air with pleasure

Obviously, there are many, many ways you could give a presentation about cheese, but this was just a quick look at how you can take a topic and put something together.

It is really FUN – give it a try.

Topic: _____

Specific Message: _____

_____

Introduction

1. _____

2. _____

3. _____

Body

Point 1:_____

1. _____

2. _____

3. _____

Point 2:_____

1. _____

2. _____

3. _____

Point 3: _____

1. _____

2. _____

3. _____

<u>**Conclusion**</u>

1. _____

2. _____

3. _____

Don't forget to consider your transition statements and audience.

I always try to leave my audience in a better place after the presentation than where they were when we started. After this exercise, don't you feel empowered? ☺

Notes and Key Points From This Chapter:

_____

_____

_____

_____

_____

_____

_____

_____

_____

_____

_____

_____

_____

_____

_____

Chapter Seventeen
A Variety of Structures

After you have determined what you are going to say, there are several ways to put the information together.

In Chapters Three and Sixteen we discussed a basic structure for an effective presentation. In Chapter Two, using the OREO method, we looked at an effective structure for impromptu speaking, but there are several other structure options that can be used for a very effective presentation. In this chapter, we will look at a few more of these options.

As we are going through these different structures, keep in mind that we are talking about the structure for the *body* of the presentation. We still need an introduction to introduce the topic to the audience, and a conclusion to wrap up the information. These structures are designed to help you think of other ways to put the information together.

Also, the structure does not have to be related to the type of speech (Informing, Persuading, Motivating, Inspiring, and Entertaining).

To more clearly illustrate the point, let's use the same topic for the first three structures.

Straight Information – when giving information is your primary goal. You may still use the three point method that we have discussed, but the points do not have to be in a specific order.

Example – Topic is Coffee:
     1. Where it is grown
     2. How much is consumed daily
     3. Ways to make coffee

Comparison – comparing two situations or events or items and indicating their similarities.

Example – Topic is Coffee and Tea:
1. Both caffeinated products
2. Can be consumed hot or cold
3. High quality availability

Contrast – contrasting two situations or events or items and indicting their differences.

Example – Topic is Coffee and Tea:
1. Bean vs. leaf
2. Origin of production – Brazil vs. India or China
3. Different medicinal uses

Cause/Effect – in this structure there is a cause that created an effect or a relationship between two events with a specific result.

Example – Topic is: Environmental Pollution and the Possible Effects on Global Warming
OR
Example – Topic is: Better Financial Planning Provides for a More Secure Future

Problem/Solution – identifying the problem and offering a solution or solutions.

Example – Topic is: Traffic congestion in the Metropolitan areas can be reduced by greater use of mass transit options.

If you want to use the three point system with the problem/solution structure, you could identify three ways to reduce congestion, or three "solutions", you could use:
1. Carpool – share a ride
2. Bus transportation
3. Flexible work hours

You will note that we did not identify three main points in a few of these examples, as it isn't always necessary, just an effective option.

Timeline or Sequence of Events – when a timeline or sequence of events is important to the situation. These presentations often have multiple points. This is a great structure to use when you are talking about historical events or when reporting on the progress of a project.

When using this structure, it is common to have more than 3-5 points in your presentation. The mind is still most comfortable when recalling 3-5 points, but the added image of a timeline, especially when backed up with a clear, concise visual aid, will help your audience to recall more than 3-5 points. Often this structure is used to offer an historic perspective, and it isn't imperative for your audience to be able to recall all of the points, just the fact that whatever you are talking about has spanned a period of time or sequence of events.

Example – Topic is: Olympic Games

Greece in 776 BC - Olympic games begin in Athens.

Athens 1896 – Modern games begin as England, Greece, Italy, Russia, Spain, Sweden and the United States open Games. Tradition of honoring victor and his/her country by the playing of their country's anthem is started.

Paris 1900 - Games opened to women.

Stockholm 1912 - First use of electronic timing devices and a public address system.

Antwerp 1920 - Olympic flag unfurled for first time; its five colored rings (black, blue, yellow, green and red) incorporate at least one color found in the flag of every nation on earth.

Los Angeles 1932 - 16 world records and 33 Olympic records set.

Helsinki 1952 - Soviet Union rejoins Games after 40-year absence.

Tokyo 1964 - Opening ceremonies broadcast via satellite to U. S. for first time.

And we could go on and on with the locations, dates and important events at each location. You most likely do not expect your audience to remember all of the points on the timeline, but you can clearly indicate the span of time from the beginning to the present.

There are also many presentations you could give on the individual athletes who have participated in the Olympics. Some of their stories are just incredible, including Wilma Rudolph, one of 22 children, born premature and faced many ailments including polio at a young age. Her parents were told she would never walk. At age 12 she walked unassisted for the first time in her life and at age 16 she started an Olympic/Athletic career that broke gender and racial barriers and set records for track and field events. Her story is just one of the truly inspiring stories of Olympic athletes.

You could also use this topic for the next structure of *Time in Threes*.

Time in Threes – when the structure is best suited for a relationship between past, present and future

Example – Topic is: Introduce Yourself
　　　1. My past life
　　　2. My present life
　　　3. My future plans
OR

Example – Topic is: Automobile Transportation through the Years
    1. Gasoline powered engines
    2. Hybrid and fuel efficient vehicles
    3. Futuristic automobile plans

Whole in Pieces – when you are describing putting something together, but the order in which you put it together is not important.

Example – Baking a cake where all the ingredients go into the pan without a specific order. Some refer to this as a "dump cake" because you are just "dumping" the ingredients in the pan and it does not matter in which order you place the items.

This structure is related to the straight information structure, but this structure is more appropriate when you are assembling something.

This is where I always put in the story about my friend Carol and her cake baking. If you missed it, check out the end of Chapter Eleven.

Ordered Steps – when you are describing putting something together, but the order is important to the outcome.

Example – Topic is Refinishing Furniture
    1. Remove old varnish
    2. Clean the item thoroughly
    3. Apply new varnish

This may seem like a simple example, but the point is that you should not put the new varnish on before taking the old varnish off and cleaning the item.

As you can see, there are several structure options available to make the most effective presentation.

Notes and Key Points From This Chapter:

_____

_____

_____

_____

_____

_____

_____

_____

_____

_____

_____

_____

_____

_____

_____

Chapter Eighteen
Image Mapping for Presenters

In the world of computers, there is a technique called image mapping that allows a user to click on a part of an image and be taken to another image or informational link. In essence, this allows the use of various parts to make up a whole.

In the previous chapter on different structures, we looked at a lot of ways to put a presentation together. This section offers another idea, something I call **Image Mapping for Presenters**. We will look at a sample from a presentation and how it uses this structure for great effectiveness. This is different than the Mind Mapping that we discuss from Tony Buzan, (next chapter) in that you think of just the image and that is what directs your presentation.

The topic is Leadership. In this *original presentation* on leadership, titled, *Engaging the Whole Body of Leadership*, I use a simple hand-out with the image below as the "image" for the presentation structure:

This funny looking image (I couldn't even draw a good stick figure, but I can put pieces together thanks to clip art), is on the front of the hand-out. On the back of the hand-out, I have a list of body parts (head, eyes, nose, legs, etc.) and blank lines beside each word for note taking. In most of my presentations, I try to make the hand-outs very simple. This allows the listener to take notes from the presentation related to what they find most helpful.

I start the presentation out with the children's song, "Head, Shoulders, Knees and Toes", and have the audience stand and sing with me. From there I start talking about engaging the whole body as an effective leader. The "image" of the body helps guide my presentation as I start with the:

> **Head** – a leader must **think** themselves a leader to start the process. I also talk about an effective leader understanding that there are many parts of being a good leader, not just getting the job done. An effective leader must also understand the human element and hopefully when they put their head on the pillow at night, it will be for a restful sleep.

From there we move to the:

> **Eyes** – an effective leader must have a vision. If I am doing this in the corporate setting, I read the Vision Statement from the company and discuss the key words used in the Vision Statement and what that means for effective leadership.

From there the **Mouth** (communication), etc…

By using this Image Mapping concept, as a speaker you could look at the image and recall the points that you want to discuss very easily. The same type of structure could be used with other items, for example, a clock discussing time management where you could use the numbers at three, six, nine, and twelve as your four points, or even a twelve point list. You could use any image related to your topic, for example, Ted Corcoran, author of **The Leadership Bus** uses the image of a bus when talking about leadership.

There is an **added bonus** in this chapter with this type of presentation structure that you may find very helpful. In the presentation on leadership I use a lot of quotes relating to the topic. As we discussed in great detail in Chapter Twelve, quotes can be a great foundation for a presentation.

During this presentation, I state all of the quotes a couple of times for emphasis, and I also make sure my web site address is on the hand-out. I tell my audience that they can go to my web site and get the complete list of quotes used during the presentation. This is an added marketing tool to get your audience to check out more information on your web site.

When you are using a quote in a presentation, it is very important to be accurate with the quote and cite the source. It is quite acceptable to read the quote for accuracy. Since this session has several quotes on leadership, I have assigned at least one quote for each body part. To make sure I have the quote correct, I have it written on a numbered (very important) index card with the body part listed, the quote and author, and one or two key words that I want to make sure I have talked about with each point.

By using the index cards in this manner, I am sure to get the quote and author correct, as well as a quick reminder of the key elements (personally, I use brightly colored cards so I can find them easier in the white paper world, and I love bright colors). It takes just a few seconds to read the card and glance at the key phrases. For example, the card for Head has the number 1 in the right corner (as it is the first body part I discuss) it has two words – THINK and PILLOW, then a couple of quotes. In this instance, the quotes are:

"Management is doing things right; leadership is doing the right things." — Peter Drucker

"You do not lead by hitting people over the head, that is assault, not leadership." — Dwight D. Eisenhower

The numbers in the corner are a quick reminder and will also help me keep things in order should the cards fall on the floor before the presentation.

In this example, the key element is the Image Mapping for Presenters structure. The quotes add to the presentation, but I can certainly give the presentation without ALL of the quotes – many I simply remember because I have given the presentation multiple times. The image is what provides the structure to follow as I work my way through the body parts. This concept can be very helpful in many situations, and I have used it on more than one occasion when a last minute presentation was needed at a meeting or conference.

Image Mapping for Presenters Exercise: Using the Image Mapping for Presenters structure, identify "images" with which you are familiar that you can use as the basis for a presentation.

1. _____

      Point 1: _____

      Point 2: _____

      Point 3: _____

2. _____

      Point 1: _____

      Point 2: _____

      Point 3: _____

3. _____

      Point 1: _____

      Point 2: _____

      Point 3: _____

4. _____

      Point 1: _____

      Point 2: _____

      Point 3: _____

Notes and Key Points From This Chapter:

_____

_____

_____

_____

_____

_____

_____

_____

_____

_____

_____

_____

_____

_____

_____

_____

Chapter Nineteen
Mapping Your Talk

By now we have discussed several techniques that can help you decide what to say in a presentation. People generally fall into two categories – 1) I don't have anything to say, or 2) I have so much to talk about, and I don't know how to narrow it down. For either situation, a concept known as Mind-Mapping can help.

Mind Mapping

Mind Mapping is not a new concept for brainstorming. Tony Buzan is considered to be the creator and expert on Mind Mapping. He has written many books on ways to use Mind Mapping for presentations, note taking, memory development, writing, etc. His many titles include, *Use Your Head, The Mind Map Book, and Use Your Memory*, just to name a few. He has also developed Mind Mapping Software, if you choose to use the computer when developing presentation ideas using this method. To get a better understanding of his work, pick up one of his books and start fully mapping your mind.

Mr. Buzan's work includes diagrams, dynamic colors, expressive pictures, and several different styles of maps. For our purposes in this book, we will look at the Mind Map in the most simplistic form. On the following pages, you can see some very simple mind map examples, plus blank diagrams as a guide for your next presentation.

In Example 1, we will use a more common topic and break it down. If we want to talk about sports, we have many, many types of sports from which to choose. Begin by placing the topic in the center of the diagram, then listing as many categories of that topic on the lines around the center circle.

For each of the sub-categories, you can choose additional categories, again placing them on lines extending from the sub-categories line, and continue this process until you have exhausted all of your ideas. Due to limited space, we have used just the basics for this example, but you can easily see that a category as broad as Sports could generate hundreds of presentation ideas.

Example 1 – Using a Main Category

Example 2 – Using a Sub-Category

If you have too much material, the next step would be to take one individual sub-category, make that the main category and continue to develop more topics.

Example 2 uses one of the arms of the mind map and breaks it down again into several topics you could use for a presentation.

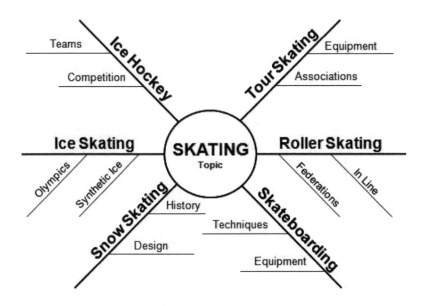

For this example, I purposely used a category of SPORTS; a category of which I know little about, to indicate further how much information is out there from which you can choose. With a little searching your topics are almost limitless.

The Mind Map method, even in this simple form, can help you collect your brainstorming thoughts in a more organized manner than just putting them on paper. Use the following templates to map a few ideas you may have and discover how you can enhance limited information that you may have on the topic, or narrow down too much information.

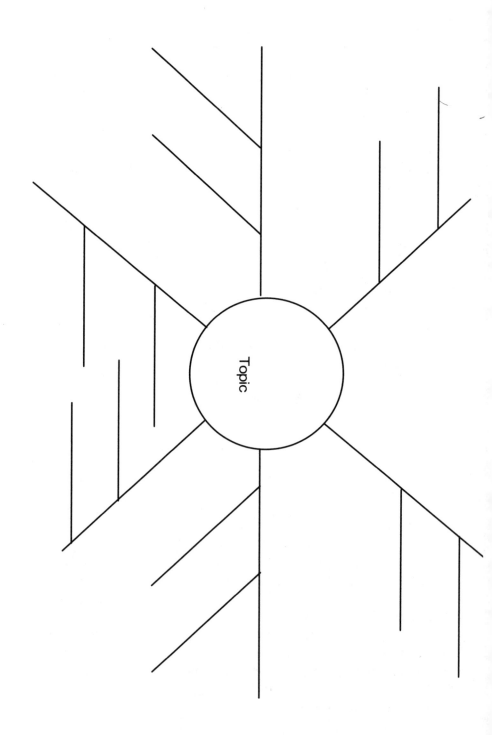

Topic

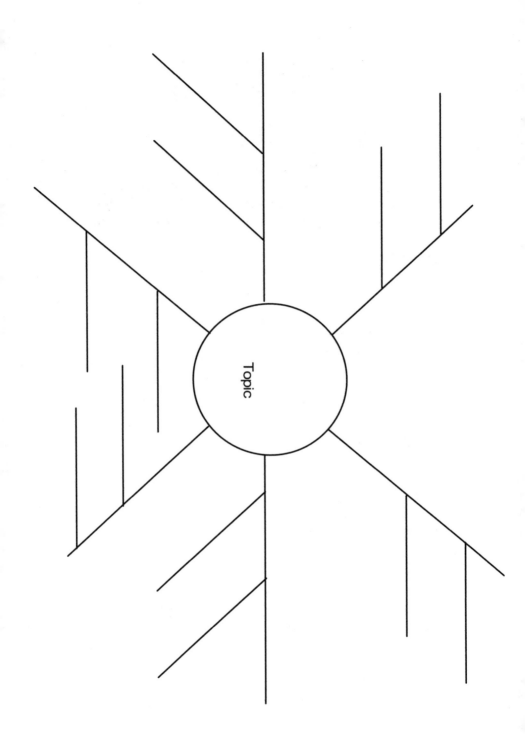

Chapter Twenty
Tiers to Talking

Another method for determining what to talk about is what I call using a Topic Tier. The Topic Tier is designed to think in a more structured method than the Mind Map. To make a good comparison, let's look at the same topics as before, but this time use the Topic Tiers method. There are blanks provided for you to fill in your own Topic Tiers for your topics.

Topic is Sports

1. Football

    A. U.S. Football
    B. Soccer

2. Skating

    A. Ice Skating
    B. Roller Skating

3. Basketball

    A. Associations
    B. Hall of Fame

4. Tennis

    A. Table
    B. Court
        1. Clay
        2. Grass
        3. Indoor

5. Golf
    A. Rules
    B. Championships

6. Baseball

    A. World Series
    B. Leagues

7. Boxing

    A. History
    B. Terminology

Topic is Skating as a Sub-Category

1. Tour Skating

    A. Equipment
    B. Associations

2. Roller Skating
    A. In Line
    B. Federation

3. Skateboarding

    A. Techniques
    B. Equipment

4. Snow Skating

    A. History
    B. Design

5. Ice Skating

    A. Olympics
    B. Synthetic Ice

6. Ice Hockey
    A. Teams
    B. Competitions

Topic Tiers

Topic: _____

1. _____
   A. _____
   B. _____
   C. _____

2. _____
   A. _____
   B. _____
   C. _____

3. _____
   A. _____
   B. _____
   C. _____

4. _____
   A. _____
   B. _____
   C. _____

5. _____
   A. _____
   B. _____
   C. _____

6. _____
   A. _____
   B. _____
   C. _____

7. _____
   A. _____
   B. _____
   C. _____

8. _____
   A. _____
   B. _____
   C. _____

9. _____
   A. _____
   B. _____
   C. _____

Topic Tiers

Topic: _____

1. _____
   A. _____
   B. _____
   C. _____

2. _____
   A. _____
   B. _____
   C. _____

3. _____
   A. _____
   B. _____
   C. _____

4. _____
   A. _____
   B. _____
   C. _____

5. _____
   A. _____
   B. _____
   C. _____

6. _____
   A. _____
   B. _____
   C. _____

7. _____
   A. _____
   B. _____
   C. _____

8. _____
   A. _____
   B. _____
   C. _____

9. _____
   A. _____
   B. _____
   C. _____

Appendix A
<u>Top 10 List – Before You Speak</u>

This book is dedicated to looking at ways to decide *what to say* and *how to say it*, but there are a lot of other elements that go into a fantastic presentation. As I mentioned, we did not look at the actual delivery techniques of a presentation. My next book, *How to Deliver Life as Speech Material* ☺ will look closer at effective delivery techniques. However, there are several factors that a speaker must take into consideration in addition to what we covered in this book. Here is a quick Top 10 List to consider.

1. Know Yourself – Who are you and what do you want to talk about? Be comfortable with the material from an ethics and value viewpoint. Believe in what you are saying. The best presentations come from the heart!

2. Know Your Audience – Reinforcing it in this list, a must for relating your information – review Chapter Four.

3. Practice Your Material – Own it. Make sure you know what you are talking about and then start talking. I do not recommend memorizing your entire presentation as there is great value is "being fresh" when delivering your information.

4. Know Your Room – Whenever possible, check out the room before you speak to understand the layout, equipment, lighting, and sound, and know how to operate it and make sure you have the contact person in case there is a question.

5. See Yourself as a Success – The mind is extremely powerful as we see ourselves succeeding. Visualize your success. The people in the audience want to see you succeed. Believe it and you will achieve it.

6. Breathe and Relax – When you are speaking, remember, this is one presentation in one life time. *Most* presentations do not determine life and death. A clear, relaxed mind is much more effective.

7. Don't Apologize to the Audience – If you have forgotten something, there is a good chance your audience does not know it – don't tell them. If it is a major point, then your practicing will give you an advantage in how to weave the forgotten information into the presentation. If it isn't a major part, then the audience most likely will not know that you are "missing" anything.

8. Go With the Flow – Situations may arise regarding the equipment, the room, or the audience. Be ready for anything. Control what you can control, but also understand that there are things that you cannot control. Experience will help you deal with those unexpected situations.

9. Gain Experience – Speak up every chance you get to add value – in a meeting; with a group of friends; any place you can speak. If you aren't already a Toastmaster, join a club. It is a great experience with fantastic feedback, no matter what level of speaking you are doing or would like to do.

10. Have FUN! – Simple stated - life is too short not to have fun! Don't forget to laugh and remember that you cannot always change the situation, but you *can* control how you respond. Live your life…Love your life…and talk about it! Life is indeed just speech material!

May your path always be blessed with GREAT speech material!

Notes and Key Points From This Chapter:

Appendix B
Please Hand Me the Microphone

Now that you have all of this great information, where do you find your audience?

Toastmasters International

Throughout this book you have noticed multiple references to Toastmasters International and with good reason – this organization has changed my life, and it may change yours.

Toastmasters International is the world's leading organization on communication and leadership skills. Started in 1924 by Dr. Ralph Smedley, Toastmasters has grown to over 90 countries world wide, over 12,000 clubs, and over 250,000 members. When you step into a Toastmasters club, you will find a very supportive group of people to help you build or enhance your communication and leadership skills. **It is a very low-cost, highly effective way to change your life, and you have an audience.**

I have had the great honor to represent this organization in a lot of different ways through the years, including serving as an International Director. Part of that responsibility included going to businesses and organizations and discussing how Toastmasters could help the company with the communication and leadership building needs for their employees. I always take great pleasure in highlighting the high quality educational program Toastmasters offers by showing the basic manuals for communication and leadership, but I am also quick to point out that I can present the great manuals and talk about the structure of the program, but what I can't show them, but know it will happen, is the greater level of confidence their employees will gain through the program. This confidence will transfer to all areas of a person's life.

If you are interested in Toastmasters International, or know someone who is, please direct them to the Toastmasters web site at: www.toastmasters.org.

National Speakers Association

Toastmasters will help you build valuable foundational skills for speaking and leading. When you are ready to take the next step and be a professional speaker or trainer, the National Speakers Association will provide you with valuable resources and information to help you achieve your goals. Check them out at: http://www.nsaspeaker.org.

Community

There are many opportunities to speak in your own community. Your religious affiliations, schools, community groups, and organizations can all benefits from someone with effective communication skills. Most organizations such as Rotary International, Lions Club, Kiwanis, Eagles, Elks, Veterans locations, and many more community minded organizations are often looking for quality speakers for their meeting agendas. No matter where you live in the world, there are opportunities in your community to make a difference. Check out your community and get started.

Remember, you just never know where your skill in speaking will take you... *You just never know what you are being prepared for!*

It is my hope that the information in this book will help you become a better communicator, a better speaker, and maybe even a better thinker and writer. It is my strong desire that the valuable skills you gain will help you for the rest of your life. As we both know, **My Life is Just Speech Material, but more importantly so is yours!**

Resource Section

Toastmasters International
Become the Speaker & Leader You Want to Be
www.toastmasters.org

National Speakers Association
NSA is the leading professional association for speakers, providing resources and education designed to advance the skills, integrity and value of its members and the speaking profession.
http://www.nsaspeaker.org

Ted Corcoran
President Toastmasters International 2003/04
Author of **The Leadership Bus**
tedc@theleadershipbus.com
www.theleadershipbus.com

Dilip R. Abayasekara, Ph.D., Accredited Speaker
Speaker Services Unlimited
Unleashing Your Communication & Performance Potential
Past International President, Toastmasters International
www.drdilip.com

Helen Blanchard
First Woman President of Toastmasters International
Toastmasters International President 1985-86
Author of **Breaking the Ice**
http://helenblanchard.com

Jamey & Molly French
jfrench1@woh.rr.com
www.mjfrench.blogspot.com

Rebecca Lamperski, Author/Speaker
Author of *In Full Bloom*
Rebecca@fullbloomppc.com
www.fullbloomppc.com

Lance Miller
2005 World Champion of Public Speaking
1418 Wabasso Way
Glendale CA 91208
(818) 243-0585
Lance@LanceMillerSpeaks.com
www.LanceMillerSpeaks.com

Sheryl Roush, President
CEO Sparkle Presentations, Inc.
Professional Speaker and Coach
http://www.sparklepresentations.com/

Craig Valentine
1999 World Champion of Public Speaking
Author of *World Class Speaking* and *The Nuts and Bolts of Public Speaking*
www.CraigValentine.com

World Laughter Tour
Steve Wilson, MA, CSP
Information, Ideas, and News for Success in Bringing Laughter to Life
http://www.worldlaughtertour.com/

Association for Applied and Therapeutic Humor (AATH)
Dedicated to the understanding, development and the clinical application of therapeutic humor.
www.aath.org/

Are you looking for a speaker for your next event, or a speech coach to take your speaking to the next level? Tammy will bring her high level of energy, enthusiasm and engagement to your event.

Contact Tammy at:
Tammy A. Miller
1172 Ghaner Road
Port Matilda, PA 16870
(814) 360-4031

E-mail: tammy@tammyspeaks.com
Web Site: www.tammyspeaks.com

A *sample* of some of the workshops and keynotes that Tammy presents:

Discovering the Healing Value of Humor
Finding Your Inner Cluck
Your Guide to Winning Presentations
Brain Aerobics
Engaging the Whole Body of Leadership
The Magic of Motivation
This Funny Place Called Work

Tammy is also the author of, **The Lighter Side of Breast Cancer Recovery: Lessons Learned Along the Path to Healing**. A little about this book…
The Lighter Side of Breast Cancer Recovery: Lessons Learned Along the Path to Healing, takes you down the path with a woman who has been there, but it may not be the path that most people follow. From surgeons equipped with clown noses, to going through surgery wearing a feather boa, Tammy looks at this very serious topic with a lighthearted attitude and some words of encouragement for others facing a difficult journey.

Check out www.tammyspeaks.com for more details.

Notes: